Götz von Berlichingen with the Iron Hand. A Drama.

Written by
Johann Wolfgang Von Goethe

Translated by
Hjalmar Hjorth Boyesen

2015

Table of Contents

DRAMATIS PERSONÆ

MAXIMILIAN,	*Emperor of Germany.*
GOETZ VON BERLICHINGEN,	*a free knight of the empire.*
ELIZABETH,	*his wife.*
MARIA,	*his sister.*
CHARLES,	*his son — a boy.*
GEORGE,	*his page.*
BISHOP OF BAMBERG.	
ADELBERT VON WEISLINGEN,	*a free German knight of the empire.*
ADELAIDE VON WALLDORF,	*widow of the* COUNT VON WALLDORF.
LIEBTRAUT,	*a courtier of the Bishop's.*
ABBOT OF FULDA,	*residing at the Bishop's court.*
OLEARIUS,	*a doctor of laws.*
BROTHER MARTIN,	*a monk.*
HANS VON SELBITZ, }	*Free knights, in alliance with* GOETZ.
FRANZ VON SICKINGEN, }	
LERSE,	*a trooper.*
FRANCIS,	*esquire to* WEISLINGEN.
Female Attendant on ADELAIDE.	
President,	*Accuser and Avenger of the Secret Tribunal.*
METZLER, }	
SIEVERS, }	
LINK, }	*Leaders of the insurgent peasantry.*
KOHL, }	
WILD, }	

Imperial Commissioners.

Two Merchants of Nuremberg.

Magistrates of Heilbronn.

Maximilian Stumf, a vassal of the Palsgrave.

An unknown.

Bride's father, }

Bride, } Peasants.

Bridegroom, }

Gypsy captain.

Gypsy mother and women.

Sticksand Wolf, gypsies.

Imperial captain.

Imperial officers.

Innkeeper.

Sentinel.

Sergeant-at-arms.

Imperial soldiers—Troopers belonging toGOETZ,toSELBITZ,toSICKINGENand toWEISLINGEN—Peasants—Gypsies—Judges of the Secret Tribunal—Gaolers—Courtiers, etc., etc., etc.

ACT I.

SCENE I. —

An Inn at Schwarzenberg in Franconia.
[METZLER*and*SIEVERS,*two Swabian*PEASANTS,*are seated at a table — At the fire, at some distance from them, two*TROOPERS*from Bamberg — The*INNKEEPER.

Sievers.
Hänsel! Another cup of brandy — and Christian measure.

Innkeeper.
Thou art a Never-enough.

Metzler.
*(Apart to*SIEVERS.) Repeat that again about Berlichingen. — The Bambergers there are so angry they are almost black in the face.

Sievers.
Bambergers! — What are they about here?

Metzler.
Weislingen has been two days up yonder at the castle with the Earl — they are his attendants — they came with him, I know not whence; they are waiting for him — he is going back to Bamberg.

Sievers.
Who is that Weislingen?

Metzler.
The Bishop of Bamberg's right hand! a powerful lord, who is lying in wait to play Goetz some trick.

Sievers.
He had better take care of himself.

Metzler.

(Aside.) Prithee go on! *(Aloud.)* How long is it since Goetz had a new dispute with the bishop? I thought all had been agreed and squared between them.

Sievers.

Ay! Agreement with priests!—When the bishop saw he could do no good, and always got the worst of it, he pulled in his horns, and made haste to patch up a truce—and honest Berlichingen yielded to an absurd extent, as he always does when he has the advantage.

Metzler.

God bless him! a worthy nobleman.

Sievers.

Only think! Was it not shameful? They fell upon a page of his, to his no small surprise; but they will soon be mauled for that.

Metzler.

How provoking that his last stroke should have missed. He must have been plaguily annoyed.

Sievers.

I don't think anything has vexed him so much for a long time. Look you, all had been calculated to a nicety; the time the bishop would come from the bath, with how many attendants, and which road; and had it not been betrayed by some traitor, Goetz would have blessed his bath for him, and rubbed him dry.

First Trooper.

What are you prating there about our bishop; do you want to pick a quarrel?

Sievers.

Mind your own affairs; you have nothing to do with our table.

Second Trooper.

Who taught you to speak disrespectfully of our bishop?

Sievers.

Am I bound to answer *your* questions?—Look at the fool!

[*The first*TROOPER*boxes his ears.*

Metzler.

Smash the rascal!

[*They attack each other.*

Second Trooper.

(*To* METZLER.) Come on if you dare —

Innkeeper.

(*Separating them.*) Will you be quiet? Zounds! Take yourself off if you have any scores to settle; in my house I will have order and decency. (*He pushes the* TROOPERS *out of doors.*) — And what are you about, you jackasses?

Metzler.

No bad names, Hänsel! or your sconce shall pay for it. Come, comrade, we'll go and thrash those blackguards.

Enter two of BERLICHINGEN'S TROOPERS.

First Trooper.

What's the matter?

Sievers.

Ah! Good-day, Peter! — Good-day, Veit! — Whence come you?

Second Trooper.

Mind you don't let out whom we serve.

Sievers.

(*Whispering.*) Then your master Goetz isn't far off?

First Trooper.

Hold your tongue! — Have you had a quarrel?

Sievers.

You must have met the fellows without — they are Bambergers.

First Trooper.

What brings them here?

Sievers.

They escort Weislingen, who is up yonder at the castle with the Earl.

First Trooper.

Weislingen!

Second Trooper.

(*Aside to his companion.*) Peter, that is grist to our mill. How long has he been here?

Metzler.

Two days—but he is off to-day, as I heard one of his fellows say.

First Trooper.

(*Aside.*) Did I not tell you he was here?—We might have waited yonder long enough. Come, Veit—

Sievers.

Help us first to drub the Bambergers.

Second Trooper.

There are already two of you—We must away—Farewell!

[*Exeunt both*TROOPERS.

Sievers.

Scurvy dogs, these troopers!

They won't strike a blow without pay.

Metzler.

I could swear they have something in hand.—Whom do they serve?

Sievers.

I am not to tell—they serve Goetz.

Metzler.

So!—Well, now we'll cudgel those fellows outside. While I have a quarter-staff I care not for their spits.

Sievers.

If we durst but once serve the princes in the same manner, who drag our skins over our ears!

[*Exeunt.*

SCENE II.—

A Cottage in a thick Forest.

[GOETZ VON BERLICHINGEN*discovered walking among the trees before the door.*

Goetz.

Where linger my servants?—I must walk up and down, or sleep will overcome me—five days and nights already on the watch. It is hardly earned, this bit of life and freedom. But when I have caught thee, Weislingen, I shall take my ease. *(Fills a glass of wine and drinks; looks at the flask.)* — Again empty. — George! — While this and my courage last, I can laugh at the ambition and chicanery of princes! — George! — You may send round your obsequious Weislingen to your uncles and cousins to calumniate my character — be it so — I am on the alert. — Thou hast escaped me, bishop; then thy dear Weislingen shall pay the score. — George! — Doesn't the boy hear? — George! George!

George.

(Entering in the cuirass of a fullgrown man.) Worshipful sir.

Goetz.

What kept you? Were you asleep? — What in the devil's name means this masquerade? — Come hither; you don't look amiss. Be not ashamed, boy; you look bravely. Ah! if you could but fill it! — Is it Hans' cuirass?

George.

He wished to sleep a little, and unbuckled it.

Goetz.

He takes things easier than his master.

George.

Do not be angry! I took it quietly away and put it on, then fetched my father's old sword from the wall, ran to the meadow, and drew it —

Goetz.

And laid about you, no doubt? — Rare times for the brambles and thorns! — Is Hans asleep?

George.

He started up and cried out to me when you called — I was trying to unbuckle the cuirass when I heard you twice or thrice.

Goetz.

Go take back his cuirass, and tell him to be ready with his horses.

George.

I have fed them well and they are ready bridled; you may mount when you will.

Goetz.

Bring me a stoup of wine. Give Hans a glass too, and tell him to be on the alert—there is good cause; I expect the return of my scouts every moment.

George.

Ah! noble sir!

Goetz.

What's the matter?

George.

May I not go with you?

Goetz.

Another time, George! when we waylay merchants and seize their wagons—

George.

Another time!—You have said that so often.—Oh, this time, this time! I will only skulk behind; just keep on the lookout—I will gather up all the spent arrows for you.

Goetz.

Next time, George!—You must first have a doublet, a steel cap and a lance.

George.

Take me with you now!—Had I been with you last time, you would not have lost your cross-bow.

Goetz.

Do you know about that?

George.

You threw it at your antagonist's head; one of his followers picked it up, and off with it he went.—Don't I know about it?

Goetz.

Did my people tell you?

George.

Oh, yes: and for that I whistle them all sorts of tunes while we dress the horses, and teach them merry songs, too.

Goetz.

Thou art a brave boy.

George.

Take me with you to prove myself so.

Goetz.

The next time, I promise you! You must not go to battle unarmed as you are. There is a time coming which will also require men. I tell thee, boy, it will be a dear time. Princes shall offer their treasures for a man whom they now hate. Go, George, give Hans his cuirass again, and bring me wine. (*Exit*GEORGE.) Where can my people be? It is incomprehensible! — A monk! What brings him here so late?
*Enter Brother*MARTIN.

Goetz.

Good-evening, reverend father! Whence come you so late? Man of holy rest, thou shamest many knights.

Martin.

Thanks, noble sir! I am at present but an unworthy brother, if we come to titles. My cloister name is Augustin, but I like better to be called by my Christian name, Martin.

Goetz.

You are tired, brother Martin, and doubtless thirsty.
*Enter*GEORGE*with wine.*

Goetz.

Here, in good time, comes wine!

Martin.

For me a draught of water. I dare not drink wine.

Goetz.

Is it against your vow?

Martin.

Noble sir, to *drink* wine is not against my vow; but because *wine* is against my vow, therefore I drink it not.

Goetz.

How am I to understand that?

Martin.

'Tis well for thee that thou dost not understand it. Eating and drinking nourish man's life.

Goetz.

Well!

Martin.

When thou hast eaten and drunken, thou art as it were new born, stronger, bolder, fitter for action. Wine rejoices the heart of man, and joyousness is the mother of every virtue. When thou hast drunk wine thou art double what thou should'st be! twice as ingenious, twice as enterprising, and twice as active.

Goetz.

As I drink it, what you say is true.

Martin.

'Tis when thus taken in moderation that I speak of it. But we —

[GEORGE*brings water.*

Goetz.

(*Aside to*GEORGE.) Go to the road which leads to Daxbach; lay thine ear close to the earth, and listen for the tread of horses. Return immediately.

Martin.

But we, on the other hand, when we have eaten and drunken, are the reverse of what we should be. Our sluggish digestion depresses our mental powers; and in the indulgence of luxurious ease, desires are generated which grow too strong for our weakness.

Goetz.

One glass, brother Martin, will not disturb your sleep. You have travelled far to-day. (*Raises his glass.*) Here's to all fighting men!

Martin.

With all my heart! (*They ring their glasses.*) I cannot abide idle people — yet will I not say that all monks are idle; they do what they can: I am just come from St. Bede, where I slept last night. The prior took me into the garden; that is their hive.

Excellent salad, cabbages in perfection, and such cauliflowers and artichokes as you will hardly find in Europe.

Goetz.

So that is not the life for you?

[*Goes out and looks anxiously after the boy. Returns.*

Martin.

Would that God had made me a gardener, or day laborer, I might then have been happy! My convent is Erfurt in Saxony; my abbot loves me; he knows I cannot remain idle, and so he sends me round the country, wherever there is business to be done. I am on my way to the Bishop of Constance.

Goetz.

Another glass. Good speed to you!

Martin.

The same to you.

Goetz.

Why do you look at me so steadfastly, brother?

Martin.

I am in love with your armor.

Goetz.

Would you like a suit? It is heavy and toilsome to the wearer.

Martin.

What is not toilsome in this world? — But to me nothing is so much so as to renounce my very nature! Poverty, chastity, obedience — three vows, each of which taken singly seems the most dreadful to humanity — so insupportable are they all; — and to spend a lifetime under this burthen, or to groan despairingly under the still heavier load of an evil conscience — ah! Sir Knight, what are the toils of your life compared to the sorrows of a state which, from a mistaken desire of drawing nearer to the Deity, condemns as crimes the best impulses of our nature, impulses by which we live, grow and prosper!

Goetz.

Were your vow less sacred I would give you a suit of armor and a steed, and we would ride out together.

Martin.

Would to Heaven my shoulders had strength to bear armor, and my arm to unhorse an enemy!—Poor weak hand, accustomed from infancy to swing censers, to bear crosses and banners of peace, how could'st thou manage the lance and falchion? My voice, tuned only to Aves and Halleluiahs, would be a herald of my weakness to the enemy, while yours would overpower him; otherwise no vows should keep me from entering an order founded by the Creator himself.

Goetz.

To your happy return.

[*Drinks.*

Martin.

I drink that only in compliment to you! A return to my prison must ever be unhappy. When you, Sir Knight, return to your castle, with the consciousness of your courage and strength, which no fatigue can overcome; when you, for the first time, after a long absence, stretch yourself unarmed upon your bed, secure from the attack of enemies, and resign yourself to a sleep sweeter than the draught after a long thirst—then can you speak of happiness.

Goetz.

And accordingly it comes but seldom.

Martin.

(*With growing ardor.*) But when it does come, it is a foretaste of paradise. When you return home laden with the spoils of your enemies, and, remember, "such a one I struck from his horse ere he could discharge his piece—such another I overthrew, horse and man;" then you ride to your castle, and—

Goetz.

And what?

Martin.

And your wife—(*Fills a glass.*) To her health! (*He wipes his eyes.*) You have one?

Goetz.

A virtuous, noble wife!

Martin.

Happy the man who possesses a virtuous wife, his life is doubled. This blessing was denied me, yet was woman the glory or crown of creation.

Goetz.

(*Aside.*) I grieve for him. The sense of his condition preys upon his heart.

Enter GEORGE, *breathless.*

George.

My lord, my lord, I hear horses in full gallop! — two of them — 'tis they for certain.

Goetz.

Bring out my steed; let Hans mount. Farewell, dear brother; God be with you. Be cheerful and patient. He will give you ample scope.

Martin.

Let me request your name.

Goetz.

Pardon me — Farewell!

[*Gives his left hand.*

Martin.

Why do you give the left? — Am I unworthy of the knightly right hand?

Goetz.

Were you the Emperor, you must be satisfied with this. My right hand, though not useless in combat, is unresponsive to the grasp of affection. It is one with its mailed gauntlet — You see, it is *iron!*

Martin.

Then art thou Goetz of Berlichingen. I thank thee, Heaven, who hast shown me the man whom princes hate, but to whom the oppressed throng! (*He takes his right hand.*) Withdraw not this hand: let me kiss it.

Goetz.

You must not!

Martin.

Let me, let me—Thou hand, more worthy even than the saintly relic through which the most sacred blood has flowed! lifeless instrument, quickened by the noblest spirit's faith in God.

[GOETZ*adjusts his helmet and takes his lance.*

Martin.

There was a monk among us about a year ago, who visited you when your hand was shot off at the siege of Landshut. He used to tell us what you suffered, and your grief at being disabled for your profession of arms; till you remembered having heard of one who had also lost a hand, and yet served long as a gallant knight—I shall never forget it.

*Enter the two*TROOPERS.*They speak apart with*GOETZ.

Martin.

(Continuing.) I shall never forget his words uttered in the noblest, the most childlike trust in God: "If I had twelve hands, what would they avail me without thy grace? then may I with only one—"

Goetz.

In the wood of Haslach then. *(Turns to*MARTIN.*)* Farewell, worthy brother!

[*Embraces him.*

Martin.

Forget me not, as I shall never forget thee!

[*Exeunt*GOETZ*and his*TROOPERS.

Martin.

How my heart beat at the sight of him. He spoke not, yet my spirit recognized his. What rapture to behold a great man!

George.

Reverend sir, you will sleep here?

Martin.

Can I have a bed?

George.

No, sir! I know of beds only by hearsay; in our quarters there is nothing but straw.

Martin.

It will serve. What is thy name?

George.

George, reverend sir.

Martin.

George! Thou hast a gallant patron saint.

George.

They say he was a trooper; that is what I intend to be!

Martin.

Stop! *(Takes a picture from his breviary and gives it to him.)* There behold him — follow his example; be brave, and fear God.

[*Exit into the cottage.*

George.

Ah! what a splendid gray horse! If I had but one like that — and the golden armor. There is an ugly dragon. At present I shoot nothing but sparrows. O St. George! make me but tall and strong; give me a lance, armor and such a horse, and then let the dragons come!

[*Exit.*

Fr. Pecht del.
PUBLISHED BY GEORGE BARRIE
[*Editor: illegible text*]
Elizabeth

SCENE III. —

An Apartment in Jaxthausen, the Castle of Goetz von Berlichingen.

ELIZABETH, MARIA*and*CHARLES*discovered.*

Charles.

Pray now, dear aunt, tell me again that story about the good child; it is so pretty —

Maria.

Do you tell it to me, little rogue! that I may see if you have paid attention.

Charles.

Wait then till I think. — "There was once upon — " Yes — "There was once upon a time a child, and his mother was sick; so the child went — "

Maria.

No, no! — "Then his mother said, 'Dear child — ' "

Charles.

" 'I am sick — ' "

Maria.

" 'And cannot go out.' "

Charles.

"And gave him money and said, 'Go and buy yourself a breakfast.' There came a poor man — "

Maria.

"The child went. There met him an old man who was — ." Now, Charles!

Charles.

"Who was — old — "

Maria.

Of course. "Who was hardly able to walk, and said, 'Dear child — ' "

Charles.

" 'Give me something; I have eaten not a morsel yesterday or to-day.' Then the child gave him the money — "

Maria.

"That should have bought his breakfast."

Charles.

"Then the old man said — "

Maria.

"Then the old man took the child by the hand — "

Charles.

"By the hand, and said — and became a fine beautiful saint — and said — 'Dear child, — ' "

Maria.

" 'The holy Virgin rewards thee for thy benevolence through me: whatever sick person thou touchest—' "

Charles.

" 'With thy hand—.' " It was the right hand, I think.

Maria.

Yes.

Charles.

" 'He will get well directly.' "

Maria.

"Then the child ran home, and could not speak for joy—"

Charles.

"And fell upon his mother's neck and wept for joy."

Maria.

"Then the mother cried. 'What is this?' and became—" Now, Charles.

Charles.

"Became—became—"

Maria.

You do not attend—"and became well. And the child cured kings and emperors, and became so rich that he built a great abbey."

Elizabeth.

I cannot understand why my husband stays. He has been away five days and nights, and he hoped to have finished his adventure so quickly.

Maria.

I have long felt uneasy. Were I married to a man who continually incurred such danger, I should die within the first year.

Elizabeth.

I thank God that he has made me of firmer stuff!

Charles.

But must my father ride out if it is so dangerous?

Maria.

Such is his good pleasure.

Elizabeth.

He must indeed, dear Charles!

Charles.

Why?

Elizabeth.

Do you not remember the last time he rode out, when he brought you those nice things?

Charles.

Will he bring me anything now?

Elizabeth.

I believe so. Listen: there was a tailor at Stutgard who was a capital archer, and had gained the prize at Cologne.

Charles.

Was it much?

Elizabeth.

A hundred dollars; and afterwards they would not pay him.

Maria.

That was naughty, eh, Charles?

Charles.

Naughty people!

Elizabeth.

The tailor came to your father and begged him to get his money for him; then your father rode out and intercepted a party of merchants from Cologne, and kept them prisoners till they paid the money. Would you not have ridden out too?

Charles.

No; for one must go through a dark thick wood, where there are gypsies and witches —

Elizabeth.

You're a fine fellow; afraid of witches!

Maria.

Charles, it is far better to live at home in your castle like a quiet Christian knight. One may find opportunities enough of doing good on one's own lands. Even the worthiest knights do more harm than good in their excursions.

Elizabeth.

Sister, you know not what you are saying. — God grant our boy may become braver as he grows up, and not take after that Weislingen, who has dealt so faithlessly with my husband.

Maria.

We will not judge, Elizabeth. — My brother is highly incensed, and so are you; I am only a spectator in the matter, and can be more impartial.

Elizabeth.

Weislingen cannot be defended.

Maria.

What I have heard of him has interested me. — Even your husband relates many instances of his former goodness and affection. — How happy was their youth when they were both pages of honor to the margrave!

Elizabeth.

That may be. But only tell me, how can a man ever have been good who lays snares for his best and truest friend? who has sold his services to the enemies of my husband; and who strives, by invidious misrepresentations, to poison the mind of our noble emperor, who is so gracious to us?

[*A horn is heard.*]

Charles.

Papa! papa! the warder sounds his horn! Joy! joy! Open the gate!

Elizabeth.

There he comes with booty!

*Enter*PETER.

Peter.

We have fought — we have conquered! — God save you, noble ladies!

Elizabeth.

Have you captured Weislingen?

Peter.

Himself, and three followers.

Elizabeth.

How came you to stay so long?
Peter.
We lay in wait for him between Nuremberg and Bamberg, but he would not come, though we knew he had set out. At length we heard of his whereabouts; he had struck off sideways, and was staying quietly with the earl at Schwarzenberg.
Elizabeth.
They would also fain make the earl my husband's enemy.
Peter.
I immediately told my master. — Up and away we rode into the forest of Haslach. And it was curious that while we were riding along that night, a shepherd was watching, and five wolves fell upon the flock and attacked them stoutly. Then my master laughed, and said, "Good luck to us all, dear comrades, both to you and us!" And the good omen overjoyed us. Just then Weislingen came riding towards us with four attendants —
Maria.
How my heart beats!
Peter.
My comrade and I, as our master had commanded, threw ourselves suddenly on him, and clung to him as if we had grown together, so that he could not move, while my master and Hans fell upon the servants and overpowered them. They were all taken, except one who escaped.
Elizabeth.
I am curious to see him. Will he arrive soon?
Peter.
They are riding through the valley, and will be here in a quarter of an hour.
Maria.
He is no doubt cast down and dejected?
Peter.
He looks gloomy enough.
Maria.
It will grieve me to see his distress!

Elizabeth.

Oh, I must get food ready. You are no doubt all hungry?

Peter.

Hungry enough, in truth.

Elizabeth.

(*To*MARIA.) Take the cellar keys and bring the best wine. They have deserved it.

[*Exit*ELIZABETH.

Charles.

I'll go too, aunt.

Maria.

Come then, boy.

[*Exeunt*CHARLES*and*MARIA.

Peter.

He'll never be his father, else he would have gone with me to the stable.

*Enter*GOETZ. WEISLINGEN, HANS*and other*TROOPERS.

Goetz.

(*Laying his helmet and sword on a table.*) Unbuckle my armor, and give me my doublet. Ease will refresh me. Brother Martin, thou saidst truly. You have kept us long on the watch, Weislingen!

[WEISLINGEN*paces up and down in silence.*

Goetz.

Be of good cheer! Come, unarm yourself! Where are your clothes? I hope nothing has been lost. (*To the attendants.*) Go, ask his servants; open the baggage and see that nothing is missing. Or I can lend you some of mine.

ARTIST: A. WAGNER.
GÖTZ VON BERLICHINGEN. ACT I.
THE CAPTURE OF WEISLINGEN.

Weislingen.

Let me remain as I am—it is all one.

Goetz.

I can give you a handsome doublet, but it is only of linen; it has grown too tight for me. I wore it at the marriage of my Lord the Palsgrave, when your bishop was so incensed at me. About a fortnight before I had sunk two of his vessels upon the Main.—I was going upstairs in the Stag at Heidelberg, with Franz von Sickingen. Before you get quite to the top there is a landing-place with iron rails—there stood the bishop, and gave his hand to Franz as he passed, and to me also as I followed close behind him. I laughed in my sleeve, and went to the Landgrave of Hanau, who was always a kind friend to me, and said, "The bishop has given me his hand, but I'll wager he did not know me." The bishop heard me, for I was speaking loud on purpose. He came to us angrily, and said, "True, I gave thee my hand, because I knew thee not." To which I answered, "I know that, my lord; and so here you have your shake of the hand back again!" The manikin grew red as a turkey-cock with spite, and he ran up into the room and complained to the Palsgrave Lewis and the Prince of Nassau. We have laughed over the scene again and again.

Weislingen.

I wish you would leave me to myself.

Goetz.

Why so? I entreat you be of good cheer. You are my prisoner, but I will not abuse my power.

Weislingen.

I have no fear of that. That is your duty as a knight.

Goetz.

And you know how sacred it is to me.

Weislingen.

I am your prisoner—the rest matters not.

Goetz.

You should not say so. Had you been taken by a prince, fettered and cast into a dungeon, your gaoler directed to drive sleep from your eyes—

*Enter*SERVANTS*with clothes.*WEISLINGEN*unarms himself. Enter*CHARLES.

Charles.

Good-morrow, papa!

Goetz.

(Kisses him.) Good-morrow, boy! How have you been this long time?

Charles.

Very well, father! Aunt says I am a good boy.

Goetz.

Does she?

Charles.

Have you brought me anything?

Goetz.

Nothing this time.

Charles.

I have learned a great deal.

Goetz.

Ay!

Charles.

Shall I tell you about the good child?

Goetz.

After dinner.

Charles.

I know something else, too.

Goetz.

What may that be?

Charles.

"Jaxthausen is a village and castle on the Jaxt, which has appertained in property and heritage for two hundred years to the Lords of Berlichingen—"

Goetz.

Do you know the Lord of Berlichingen? (CHARLES*stares at him. Aside.*) His learning is so abstruse that he does not know his own father. To whom does Jaxthausen belong?

Charles.

"Jaxthausen is a village and castle upon the Jaxt—"

Goetz.

I did not ask that. I knew every path, pass and ford about the place before ever I knew the name of the village, castle or river. — Is your mother in the kitchen?

Charles.

Yes, papa! They are cooking a lamb and turnips.

Goetz.

Do you know that too. Jack Turnspit?

Charles.

And my aunt is roasting an apple for me to eat after dinner —

Goetz.

Can't you eat it raw?

Charles.

It tastes better roasted.

Goetz.

You must have a titbit, must you? — Weislingen, I will be with you immediately. I must go and see my wife. — Come, Charles!

Charles.

Who is that man?

Goetz.

Bid him welcome. Tell him to be merry.

Charles.

There's my hand for you, man! Be merry — for the dinner will soon be ready.

Weislingen.

(*Takes up the child and kisses him.*) Happy boy! that knowest no worse evil than the delay of dinner. May you live to have much joy in your son, Berlichingen!

Goetz.

Where there is most light the shades are deepest. Yet I should thank God for it. We'll see what they are about.

[*Exit with*CHARLES*and*SERVANTS.

Weislingen.

Oh, that I could but wake and find this all a dream! In the power of Berlichingen! — from whom I had scarcely detached myself — whose remembrance I shunned like fire — whom I hoped to overpower! and he still the old true-hearted Goetz!

Gracious God! what will be the end of it? O Adelbert! Led back to the very hall where we played as children; when thou didst love and prize him as thy soul! Who can know him and hate him? Alas! I am so thoroughly insignificant here. Happy days! ye are gone. There, in his chair by the chimney, sat old Berlichingen, while we played around him, and loved each other like cherubs! How anxious the bishop and all my friends will be! Well, the whole country will sympathize with my misfortune. But what avails it? Can they give me the peace after which I strive?

Re-enter GOETZ *with wine and goblets.*

Goetz.

We'll take a glass while dinner is preparing. Come, sit down — think yourself at home! Fancy you've come once more to see Goetz. It is long since we have sat and emptied a flagon together. *(Lifts his glass.)* Come: a light heart!

Weislingen.

Those times are gone by.

Goetz.

God forbid! To be sure, we shall hardly pass more pleasant days than those we spent together at the margrave's court, when we were inseparable night and day. I think with pleasure on my youth. Do you remember the scuffle I had with the Polander, whose pomaded and frizzled hair I chanced to rub with my sleeve?

Weislingen.

It was at table; and he struck at you with a knife.

Goetz.

I gave it him, however; and you had a quarrel upon that account with his comrades. We always stuck together like brave fellows, and were the admiration of every one. *(Raises his glass.)* Castor and Pollux! It used to rejoice my heart when the margrave so called us.

Weislingen.

The Bishop of Wurtzburg first gave us the name.

Goetz.

That bishop was a learned man, and withal so kind and gentle. I shall remember as long as I live how he used to caress us, praise our friendship, and say, "Happy is the man who is his friend's twin-brother."

Weislingen.

No more of that.

Goetz.

Why not? I know nothing more delightful after fatigue than to talk over old times. Indeed, when I recall to mind how we bore good and bad fortune together, and were all in all to each other, and how I thought this was to continue forever. Was not that my sole comfort when my hand was shot away at Landshut, and you nursed and tended me like a brother? I hoped Adelbert would in future be my right hand. And now —

Weislingen.

Alas!

Goetz.

Hadst thou but listened to me when I begged thee to go with me to Brabant, all would have been well. But then that unhappy turn for court-dangling seized thee, and thy coquetting and flirting with the women. I always told thee, when thou would'st mix with these lounging, vain court sycophants, and entertain them with gossip about unlucky matches and seduced girls, scandal about absent friends, and all such trash as they take interest in — I always said, Adelbert, thou wilt become a rogue!

Weislingen.

To what purpose is all this?

Goetz.

Would to God I could forget it, or that it were otherwise! Art thou not free and nobly born as any in Germany; independent, subject to the emperor alone; and dost thou crouch among vassals? What is the bishop to thee? Granted, he is thy neighbor, and can do thee a shrewd turn; hast thou not power and friends to requite him in kind? Art thou ignorant of the dignity of a free knight, who depends only upon God, the emperor, and himself, that thou degradest thyself to be the courtier of a stubborn, jealous priest?

Weislingen.

Let me speak!

Goetz.

What hast thou to say?

Weislingen.

You look upon the princes as the wolf upon the shepherd. And can you blame them for defending their territories and property? Are they a moment secure from the unruly knights, who plunder their vassals even upon the highroads, and sack their castles and villages? Upon the other hand, our country's enemies threaten to overrun the lands of our beloved emperor, yet, while he needs the princes' assistance, they can scarce defend their own lives; is it not our good genius which at this moment leads them to devise means of procuring peace for Germany, of securing the administration of justice, and giving to great and small the blessings of quiet? And can you blame us, Berlichingen, for securing the protection of the powerful princes, our neighbors, whose assistance is at hand, rather than relying on that of the emperor, who is so far removed from us, and is hardly able to protect himself?

Goetz.

Yes, yes, I understand you. Weislingen, were the princes as you paint them, we should all have what we want. Peace and quiet! No doubt! Every bird of prey naturally likes to eat its plunder undisturbed. The general weal! If they would but take the trouble to study that. And they trifle with the emperor shamefully. Every day some new tinker or other comes to give his opinion. The emperor means well, and would gladly put things to rights; but because he happens to understand a thing readily, and by a single word can put a thousand hands into motion, he thinks everything will be as speedily and as easily accomplished. Ordinance upon ordinance is promulgated, each nullifying the last, while the princes obey only those which serve their own interest, and prate of peace and security of the empire, while they are treading under foot their weaker neighbors. I will be sworn, many a one thanks God in his heart that the Turk keeps the emperor fully employed!

ARTIST: A. WAGNER.
GÖTZ VON BERLICHINGEN. ACT I.
GÖTZ AND HIS SON CHARLES.

Weislingen.

You view things your own way.

Goetz.

So does every one. The question is, which is the right way to view them? And your plans at least shun the day.

Weislingen.

You may say what you will; I am your prisoner.

Goetz.

If your conscience is free, so are you. How was it with the general tranquillity? I remember going as a boy of sixteen with the margrave to the Imperial Diet. What harangues the princes made! And the clergy were the most vociferous of all. Your bishop thundered into the emperor's ears his regard for justice, till one thought it had become part and parcel of his being. And now he has imprisoned a page of mine, at a time when our quarrels were all accommodated, and I had buried them in oblivion. Is not all settled between us? What does he want with the boy?

Weislingen.

It was done without his knowledge.

Goetz.

Then why does he not release him?

Weislingen.

He did not conduct himself as he ought.

Goetz.

Not conduct himself as he ought? By my honor he performed his duty, as surely as he has been imprisoned both with your knowledge and the bishop's! Do you think I am come into the world this very day, that I cannot see what all this means?

Weislingen.

You are suspicious, and do us wrong.

Goetz.

Weislingen, shall I deal openly with you? Inconsiderable as I am, I am a thorn in your side, and Selbitz and Sickingen are no less so, because we are firmly resolved to die sooner than to thank any one but God for the air we breathe, or pay homage to any one but the emperor. This is why they worry me in every possible way, blacken my character with the emperor, and among my friends and neighbors, and spy about for advantage over me. They would have me out of the way at any price; that was your reason for imprisoning the page whom you knew I had despatched for intelligence: and now you say he did not conduct himself as he should do, because he would not betray my secrets. And you, Weislingen, are their tool!

Weislingen.

Berlichingen!

Goetz.

Not a word more. I am an enemy to long explanations; they deceive either the maker or the hearer, and generally both.

*Enter*CHARLES.

Charles.

Dinner is ready, father!

Goetz.

Good news! Come, I hope the company of my women folk will amuse you. You always liked the girls. Ay, ay, they can tell many pretty stories about you. Come!

[*Exeunt.*

SCENE IV. —

*The*BISHOP OF BAMBERG'S*Palace.*

[*The*BISHOP,*the*ABBOT OF FULDA, OLEARIUS, LIEBTRAUT*and*COURTIERS*at table. The dessert and wine before them.*

Bishop.

Are there many of the German nobility studying at Bologna?

Olearius.

Both nobles and citizens; and, I do not exaggerate in saying that they acquire the most brilliant reputation. It is a proverb in the university: "As studious as a German noble." For while the citizens display a laudable diligence, in order to compensate by learning for their want of birth, the nobles strive, with praiseworthy emulation, to enhance their ancestral dignity by superior attainments.

Abbot.

Indeed!

Liebtraut.

What may one not live to hear. We live and learn, as the proverb says. "As studious as a German noble." I never heard that before.

Olearius.

Yes, they are the admiration of the whole university. Some of the oldest and most learned will soon be coming back with their doctor's degree. The emperor will doubtless be happy to intrust to them the highest offices.

Bishop.

He cannot fail to do so.

Abbot.

Do you know, for instance, a young man — a Hessian? —

Olearius.

There are many Hessians with us.

Abbot.

His name is — is —. Does nobody remember it? His mother was a Von —. Oh! his father had but one eye, and was a marshal —

Liebtraut.

Von Wildenholz!

Abbot.

Right. Von Wildenholz.

Olearius.

I know him well. A young man of great abilities. He is particularly esteemed for his talent in disputation.

Abbot.

He has that from his mother.

Liebtraut.

Yes; but his father would never praise her for that quality.

Bishop.

How call you the emperor who wrote your *Corpus Juris?*

Olearius.

Justinian.

Bishop.

A worthy prince: — here's to his memory!

Olearius.

To his memory!

[*They drink.*

Abbot.

That must be a fine book.

Olearius.

It may be called a book of books; a digest of all laws; there you find the sentence ready for every case, and where the text is antiquated or obscure, the deficiency is supplied by notes, with which the most learned men have enriched this truly admirable work.

Abbot.

A digest of all laws! — Indeed! — Then the ten commandments must be in it.

Olearius.

Implicitè; not explicitè.

Abbot.

That's what I mean; plainly set down, without any explication.

Bishop.

But the best is, you tell us that a state can be maintained in the most perfect tranquillity and subordination by receiving and rightly following that statute-book.

Olearius.

Doubtless.

Bishop.

All doctors of laws!

[*They drink.*

Olearius.

I'll tell them of this abroad. (*They drink.*) Would to Heaven that men thought thus in my country.

Abbot.

Whence come you, most learned sir?

Olearius.

From Frankfort, at your eminence's service!

Bishop.

You gentlemen of the law, then, are not held in high estimation there? — How comes that?

Olearius.

It is strange enough—when I last went there to collect my father's effects, the mob almost stoned me, when they heard I was a lawyer.

Abbot.

God bless me!

Olearius.

It is because their tribunal, which they hold in great respect, is composed of people totally ignorant of the Roman law. An intimate acquaintance with the internal condition of the town, and also of its foreign relations, acquired through age and experience, is deemed a sufficient qualification. They decide according to certain established edicts of their own, and some old customs recognized in the city and neighborhood.

Abbot.

That's very right.

Olearius.

But far from sufficient. The life of man is short, and in one generation cases of every description cannot occur; our statute-book is a collection of precedents, furnished by the experience of many centuries. Besides, the wills and opinions of men are variable; one man deems right to-day what another disapproves to-morrow; and confusion and injustice are the inevitable results. Law determines absolutely, and its decrees are immutable.

Abbot.

That's certainly better.

Olearius.

But the common people won't acknowledge that; and, eager as they are after novelty, they hate any innovation in their laws which leads them out of the beaten track, be it ever so much for the better. They hate a jurist as if he were a cut-purse or a subverter of the state, and become furious if one attempts to settle among them.

Liebtraut.

You come from Frankfort? — I know the place well — we tasted your good cheer at the emperor's coronation. You say your name is Olearius — I know no one in the town of your name.

Olearius.

My father's name was Oilman; but after the example, and with the advice of many jurists, I have Latinized the name to Olearius for the decoration of the title-page of my legal treatises.

Liebtraut.

You did well to translate yourself: a prophet is not honored in his own country — in your native guise you might have shared the same fate.

Olearius.

That was not the reason.

Liebtraut.

All things have two reasons.

Abbot.

A prophet is not honored in his own country.
Liebtraut.
But do you know why, most reverend sir?
Abbot.
Because he was born and bred there.
Liebtraut.
Well, that may be one reason. The other is, because, upon a nearer acquaintance with these gentlemen, the halo of glory and honor shed around them by the distant haze totally disappears; they are then seen to be nothing more than tiny rushlights!
Olearius.
It seems you are placed here to tell pleasant truths.
Liebtraut.
As I have wit enough to discover them, I do not lack courage to utter them.
Olearius.
Yet you lack the art of applying them well.
Liebtraut.
It is no matter where you place a cupping-glass provided it draws blood.
Olearius.
Barbers are known by their dress, and no one takes offence at their scurvy jests. Let me advise you as a precaution to bear the badge of your order—a cap and bells!
Liebtraut.
Where did you take your degree? I only ask, so that, should I ever take a fancy to a fool's cap, I could at once go to the right shop.
Olearius.
You carry face enough.
Liebtraut.
And you paunch.
[*The*BISHOP*and*ABBOT*laugh.*
Bishop.

Not so warm, gentlemen! Some other subject. At table all should be fair and quiet. Choose another subject, Liebtraut.

Liebtraut.

Opposite Frankfort lies a village called Sachsenhausen—

Olearius.

(*To the*BISHOP.) What news of the Turkish expedition, your excellency?

Bishop.

The emperor has most at heart, first of all to restore peace to the empire, put an end to feuds, and secure the strict administration of justice: then, according to report, he will go in person against the enemies of his country and of Christendom. At present internal dissensions give him enough to do; and the empire, despite half a hundred treaties of peace, is one scene of murder. Franconia, Swabia, the Upper Rhine and the surrounding countries are laid waste by presumptuous and reckless knights.—And here, at Bamberg, Sickingen, Selbitz with one leg, and Goetz with the iron hand, scoff at the imperial authority.

Abbot.

If his majesty does not exert himself, these fellows will at last thrust us into sacks.

Liebtraut.

He would be a sturdy fellow indeed who should thrust the wine-butt of Fulda into a sack!

Bishop.

Goetz especially has been for many years my mortal foe, and annoys me beyond description. But it will not last long, I hope. The emperor holds his court at Augsburg. We have taken our measures, and cannot fail of success.—Doctor, do you know Adelbert von Weislingen?

Olearius.

No, your eminence.

Bishop.

If you stay till his arrival you will have the pleasure of seeing a most noble, accomplished and gallant knight.

Olearius.

He must be an excellent man indeed to deserve such praises from such a mouth.

Liebtraut.

And yet he was not bred at any university.

Bishop.

We know that. (*The* ATTENDANTS *throng to the window.*) What's the matter?

Attendant.

Färber, Weislingen's servant, is riding in at the castle-gate.

Bishop.

See what he brings. He most likely comes to announce his master.

[*Exit* LIEBTRAUT. *They stand up and drink.*

LIEBTRAUT *re-enters.*

Bishop.

What news?

Liebtraut.

I wish another had to tell it — Weislingen is a prisoner.

Bishop.

What?

Liebtraut.

Berlichingen has seized him and three troopers near Haslach. One is escaped to tell you.

Abbot.

A Job's messenger!

Olearius.

I grieve from my heart.

Bishop.

I will see the servant; bring him up — I will speak with him myself. Conduct him into my cabinet.

[*Exit* BISHOP.

Abbot.

(*Sitting down.*) Another draught, however.

[*The* SERVANTS *fill round.*

Olearius.

Will not your reverence take a turn in the garden? "Post cœnam stabis, seu passus mille meabis."
Liebtraut.
In truth, sitting is unhealthy for you. You might get an apoplexy. *(The* ABBOT *rises. Aside.)* Let me but once get him out of doors, I will give him exercise enough!
[*Exeunt.*

Fr. Pecht del
PUBLISHED BY GEORGE BARRIE
[*Editor: illegible text*]
Maria

SCENE V. —

Jaxthausen.

MARIA. WEISLINGEN.
Maria.
You love me, you say. I willingly believe it, and hope to be happy with you, and make you happy also.
Weislingen.
I feel nothing but that I am entirely thine.
[*Embraces her.*
Maria.
Softly! — I gave you one kiss for earnest, but you must not take possession of what is only yours conditionally.
Weislingen.
You are too strict, Maria! Innocent love is pleasing in the sight of Heaven, instead of giving offence.
Maria.
It may be so. But I think differently; for I have been taught that caresses are, like fetters, strong through their union, and that maidens, when they love, are weaker than Samson after the loss of his locks.

Weislingen.

Who taught you so?

Maria.

The abbess of my convent. Till my sixteenth year I was with her — and it is only with you that I enjoy happiness like that her company afforded me. She had loved, and could tell — she had a most affectionate heart. Oh! she was an excellent woman!

Weislingen.

Then you resemble her. *(Takes her hand.)* What will become of me when I am compelled to leave you?

Maria.

(Withdrawing her hand.) You will feel some regret, I hope, for I know what my feelings will be. But you must away!

Weislingen.

I know it, dearest! and I will — for well I feel what happiness I shall purchase by this sacrifice! Now, blessed be your brother, and the day on which he rode out to capture me!

Maria.

His heart was full of hope for you and himself. Farewell! he said, at his departure, I go to recover my friend.

Weislingen.

That he has done. Would that I had studied the arrangement and security of my property, instead of neglecting it, and dallying at that worthless court! — then could'st thou have been instantly mine.

Maria.

Even delay has its pleasures.

Weislingen.

Say not so, Maria, else I shall fear that thy heart is less warm than mine. True, I deserve punishment, but what hopes will brighten every step of my journey! To be wholly thine, to live only for thee and thy circle of friends far removed from the world, in the enjoyment of all the raptures which two hearts can mutually bestow. What is the favor of princes, what the applause of the universe, to such simple, yet unequalled felicity? Many have been my hopes and wishes; but this happiness surpasses them all.

Enter GOETZ.

Goetz.

Your page has returned. He can scarcely utter a word for hunger and fatigue. My wife has ordered him some refreshment. Thus much I have gathered: the bishop will not give up my page; imperial commissioners are to be appointed, and a day named upon which the matter may be adjusted. Be that as it may, Adelbert, you are free. Pledge me but your hand that you will for the future give neither open nor secret assistance to my enemies.

Weislingen.

Here I grasp thy hand. From this moment be our friendship and confidence firm and unalterable as a primary law of nature! Let me take this hand also *(takes* MARIA'S *hand)*, and with it the possession of this most noble lady.

Goetz.

May I say yes for you?

Maria.

(Timidly.) If — if it is your wish —

Goetz.

Happily our wishes do not differ on this point. Thou need'st not blush — the glance of thine eye betrays thee. Well then, Weislingen, join hands, and I say *Amen!* My friend and brother! I thank thee, sister; thou canst do more than spin flax, for thou hast drawn a thread which can fetter this wandering bird of paradise. Yet you look not quite at your ease, Adelbert. What troubles you? *I* am perfectly happy! What I but hoped in a dream I now see with my eyes, and feel as though I were still dreaming. Now my dream is explained. I thought last night that, in token of reconciliation, I gave you this iron hand, and that you held it so fast that it broke away from my arm; I started, and awoke. Had I but dreamed a little longer I should have seen how you gave me a new living hand. You must away this instant, to put your castle and property in order.

That cursed court has made you neglect both. I must call my wife. — Elizabeth!

Maria.

How overjoyed my brother is!

Weislingen.

Yet I am still more so.

Goetz.

(*To* MARIA.) You will have a pleasant residence.

Maria.

Franconia is a fine country.

Weislingen.

And I may venture to say that my castle lies in the most fertile and delicious part of it.

Goetz.

That you may, and I can confirm it. Look you, here flows the Main, around a hill clothed with cornfields and vineyards, its top crowned with a Gothic castle; then the river makes a sharp turn, and glides round behind the rock on which the castle is built. The windows of the great hall look perpendicularly down upon the river, and command a prospect of many miles in extent.

Enter ELIZABETH.

Elizabeth.

What would'st thou?

Goetz.

You too must give your hand, and say, God bless you! They are a pair.

Elizabeth.

So soon?

Goetz.

But not unexpectedly.

Elizabeth.

May you ever adore her as ardently as while you sought her hand. And then, as your love, so be your happiness!

Weislingen.

Amen! I seek no happiness but under this condition.

Goetz.

The bridegroom, my love, must leave us for awhile; for this great change will involve many smaller ones. He must first withdraw himself from the bishop's court, in order that their friendship may gradually cool. Then he must rescue his property from the hands of selfish stewards, and—but come, sister; come, Elizabeth; let us leave him; his page has no doubt private messages for him.

Weislingen.

Nothing but what you may hear.

Goetz.

'Tis needless. Franconians and Swabians! Ye are now more closely united than ever. Now we shall be able to keep the princes in check.

[*Exeunt*GOETZ, ELIZABETH, MARIA.

Weislingen.

(*Alone.*) God in heaven! And canst Thou have reserved such happiness for one so unworthy? It is too much for my heart. How meanly I depended upon wretched fools, whom I thought I was governing, upon the smile of princes, upon the homage of those around me! Goetz, my faithful Goetz, thou hast restored me to myself, and thou, Maria, hast completed my reformation. I feel free, as if brought from a dungeon into the open air. Bamberg will I never see more—will snap all the shameful bonds that have held me beneath myself. My heart expands, and never more will I degrade myself by struggling for a greatness that is denied me. He alone is great and happy who fills his own station of independence, and has neither to command nor to obey.

*Enter*FRANCIS.

Francis.

God save you, noble sir! I bring you so many salutations that I know not where to begin. Bamberg, and ten miles round, cry with a thousand voices, God save you!

Weislingen.

Welcome, Francis! Bring'st thou aught else?

Francis.

You are held in such consideration at court that it cannot be expressed.

Weislingen.

That will not last long.

Francis.

As long as you live; and after your death it will shine with more lustre than the brazen characters on a monument. How they took your misfortune to heart!

Weislingen.

And what said the bishop?

Francis.

His eager curiosity poured out question upon question, without giving me time to answer. He knew of your accident already; for Färber, who escaped from Haslach, had brought him the tidings. But he wished to hear every particular. He asked so anxiously whether you were wounded. I told him you were whole, from the hair of your head to the nail of your little toe.

Weislingen.

And what said he to the proposals?

Francis.

He was ready at first to give up the page and a ransom to boot for your liberty. But when he heard you were to be dismissed without ransom, and merely to give your parole that the boy should be set free, he was for putting off Berlichingen with some pretence. He charged me with a thousand messages to you, more than I can ever utter. Oh, how he harangued! It was a long sermon upon the text, "I cannot live without Weislingen!"

Weislingen.

He must learn to do so.

Francis.

What mean you? He said, "Bid him hasten; all the court waits for him."

Weislingen.

Let them wait on. I shall not go to court.
Francis.
Not go to court! My gracious lord, how comes that? If you knew what I know; could you but dream what I have seen—
Weislingen.
What ails thee?
Francis.
The bare remembrance takes away my senses. Bamberg is no longer Bamberg. An angel of heaven, in semblance of woman, has taken up her abode there, and has made it a paradise.
Weislingen.
Is that all?
Francis.
May I become a shaven friar if the first glimpse of her does not drive you frantic!
Weislingen.
Who is it, then?
Francis.
Adelaide von Walldorf.
Weislingen.
Indeed! I have heard much of her beauty.
Francis.
Heard! You might as well say I have *seen* music. So far is the tongue from being able to rehearse the slightest particle of her beauty, that the very eye which beholds her cannot drink it all in.
Weislingen.
You are mad.
Francis.
That may well be. The last time I was in her company I had no more command over my senses than if I had been drunk, or, I may rather say, I felt like a glorified saint enjoying the angelic vision! All my senses exalted, more lively and more perfect than ever, yet not one at its owner's command.
Weislingen.
That is strange!

Francis.

As I took leave of the bishop, she sat by him; they were playing at chess. He was very gracious; gave me his hand to kiss, and said much, of which I heard not a syllable, for I was looking on his fair antagonist. Her eye was fixed upon the board, as if meditating a bold move. — A touch of subtle watchfulness around the mouth and cheek. — I could have wished to be the ivory king. The mixture of dignity and feeling on her brow — and the dazzling lustre of her face and neck, heightened by her raven tresses —

Weislingen.

The theme has made you quite poetical.

Francis.

I feel at this moment what constitutes poetic inspiration — a heart altogether wrapped in one idea. As the bishop ended, and I made my obeisance, she looked up and said, "Offer to your master the best wishes of an unknown. Tell him he must come soon. New friends await him; he must not despise them, though he is already so rich in old ones." I would have answered, but the passage betwixt my heart and my tongue was closed, and I only bowed. I would have given all I had for permission to kiss but one of her fingers! As I stood thus, the bishop let fall a pawn, and in stooping to pick it up, I touched the hem of her garment. Transport thrilled through my limbs, and I scarce know how I left the room.

Weislingen.

Is her husband at court?

Francis.

She has been a widow these four months, and is residing at the court of Bamberg to divert her melancholy. You will see her; and to meet her glance is to bask in the sunshine of spring.

Weislingen.

She would not make so strong an impression on me.

Francis.

I hear you are as good as married.

Weislingen.

Would I were really so! My gentle Maria will be the happiness of my life. The sweetness of her soul beams through her mild blue eyes, and, like an angel of innocence and love, she guides my heart to the paths of peace and felicity! Pack up, and then to my castle. I will not to Bamberg, though St. Bede came in person to fetch me.

[*Exit*WEISLINGEN.

Francis.

(*Alone.*) Not to Bamberg! Heavens forbid! But let me hope the best. Maria is beautiful and amiable, and a prisoner or an invalid might easily fall in love with her. Her eyes beam with compassion and melancholy sympathy; but in thine, Adelaide, is life, fire, spirit. I would . . . I am a fool; one glance from her has made me so. My master must to Bamberg, and I also, and either recover my senses or gaze them quite away.

Fr. Pecht del
PUBLISHED BY GEORGE BARRIE
[Editor: illegible text]
Adelaide

ACT II.

SCENE I. —

Bamberg. A Hall.
[*The*BISHOP*and*ADELAIDE*(playing at chess),*LIEBTRAUT*(with a guitar),*LADIES*and*COURTIERS*(standing in groups).*
Liebtraut.
(Plays and sings.)

Armed with quiver and bow,
With his torch all aglow,
Young Cupid comes winging his flight.
Courage glows in his eyes,
As adown from the skies,
He rushes, impatient for fight.

Up! up!
On! on!
Hark! the bright quiver rings!
Hark! the rustle of wings!
All hail to the delicate sprite!

They welcome the urchin; —
Ah, maidens, beware!
He finds every bosom
Unguarded and bare
In the light of his flambeau
He kindles his darts; —
They fondle and hug him

And press to their hearts.

Adelaide.

Your thoughts are not in your game. Check to the king!

Bishop.

There is still a way of escape.

Adelaide.

You will not be able to hold out long. Check to the king!

Liebtraut.

Were I a great prince, I would not play at this game, and would forbid it at court and throughout the whole land.

Adelaide.

'Tis indeed a touchstone of the brain.

Liebtraut.

Not on that account. I would rather hear a funeral bell, the cry of the ominous bird, the howling of that snarling watch-dog, conscience; rather would I hear these through the deepest sleep, than from bishops, knights and such beasts, the eternal — Check to the king!

Bishop.

Into whose head could such an idea enter?

Liebtraut.

A man's, for example, endowed with a weak body and a strong conscience, which, for the most part, indeed, accompany each other. Chess is called a royal game, and is said to have been invented for a king, who rewarded the inventor with a mine of wealth. If this be so, I can picture him to myself. He was a minor, either in understanding or in years, under the guardianship of his mother or his wife; had down upon his chin, and flaxen hair around his temples; was pliant as a willow-shoot, and liked to play at draughts with women, not from passion, God forbid! only for pastime. His tutor, too active for a scholar, too intractable for a man of the world, invented the game, *in usum Delphini,* that was so homogeneous with his majesty — and so on.

Adelaide.

Checkmate! You should fill up the chasms in our histories, Liebtraut.

[*They rise.*

Liebtraut.

To supply those in our family registers would be more profitable. The merits of our ancestors being available for a common object with their portraits, namely, to cover the naked sides of our chambers and of our characters, one might turn such an occupation to good account.

Bishop.

He will not come, you say!

Adelaide.

I beseech you, banish him from your thoughts.

Bishop.

What can it mean?

Liebtraut.

What! The reasons may be told over like the beads of a rosary. He has been seized with a fit of compunction, of which I could soon cure him.

Bishop.

Do so; ride to him instantly.

Liebtraut.

My commission —

Bishop.

Shall be unlimited. Spare nothing to bring him back.

Liebtraut.

May I venture to use your name, gracious lady?

Adelaide.

With discretion.

Liebtraut.

That's a vague commission.

Adelaide.

Do you know so little of me, or are you oo young as not to understand in what tone you should speak of me to Weislingen?

Liebtraut.

In the tone of a fowler's whistle, I think.

Adelaide.

You will never be reasonable.

Liebtraut.

Does one ever become so, gracious lady?

Bishop.

Go! go! Take the best horse in my stable; choose your servants, and bring him hither.

Liebtraut.

If I do not conjure him hither, say that an old woman who charms warts and freckles knows more of sympathy than I.

Bishop.

Yet, what will it avail? Berlichingen has wholly gained him over. He will no sooner be here than he will wish to return.

Liebtraut.

He will wish it, doubtless; but can he go? A prince's squeeze of the hand and the smiles of a beauty, from these no Weislingen can tear himself away. I have the honor to take my leave.

Bishop.

A prosperous journey!

Adelaide.

Adieu!

[*Exit*LIEBTRAUT.

Bishop.

When he is once here, I must trust to you.

Adelaide.

Would you make me your lime-twig?

Bishop.

By no means.

Adelaide.

Your call-bird then?

Bishop.

No; that is Liebtraut's part. I beseech you do not refuse to do for me what no other can.

Adelaide.

We shall see.
[*Exeunt.*

SCENE II. —

Jaxthausen. A Hall in GOETZ'S *Castle.*
Enter GOETZ *and* HANS VON SELBITZ.
Selbitz.
Every one will applaud you for declaring feud against the Nurembergers.
Goetz.
It would have eaten my very heart away had I remained longer their debtor. It is clear that they betrayed my page to the Bambergers. They shall have cause to remember me.
Selbitz.
They have an old grudge against you.
Goetz.
And I against them. I am glad they have begun the fray.
Selbitz.
These free towns have always taken part with the priests.
Goetz.
They have good reason.
Selbitz.
But we will cook their porridge for them!
Goetz.
I reckon upon you. Would that the Burgomaster of Nuremberg, with his gold chain round his neck, fell in our way, we'd astonish him with all his cleverness.
Selbitz.
I hear Weislingen is again on your side. Does he really join in our league?
Goetz.
Not immediately. There are reasons which prevent his openly giving us assistance; but for the present it is quite enough that

he is not against us. The priest without him is what the stole would be without the priest!

Selbitz.

When do we set forward?

Goetz.

To-morrow or next day. There are merchants of Bamberg and Nuremberg returning from the fair of Frankfort—we may strike a good blow.

Selbitz.

Let us hope so!

SCENE III. —

*The*BISHOP'S*Palace at Bamberg.*
ADELAIDE*and her*WAITING-MAID.

Adelaide.

He is here, sayest thou? I can scarcely believe it.

Maid.

Had I not seen him myself, I should have doubted it.

Adelaide.

The bishop should frame Liebtraut in gold for such a masterpiece of skill.

Maid.

I saw him as he was about to enter the palace. He was mounted on a gray charger. The horse started when he came on the bridge, and would not move forward. The populace thronged up the street to see him. They rejoiced at the delay of the unruly horse. He was greeted on all sides, and he thanked them gracefully all round. He sat the curvetting steed with an easy indifference, and by threats and soothing brought him to the gate, followed by Liebtraut and a few servants.

Adelaide.

What do you think of him?

Maid.

I never saw a man who pleased me so well. He is as like that portrait of the emperor as if he were his son *(pointing to a picture)*. His nose is somewhat smaller, but just such gentle light-brown eyes, just such fine light hair, and such a figure! A half melancholy expression on his face; I know not how, but he pleased me so well.

Adelaide.

I am curious to see him.

Maid.

He would be the husband for you!

Adelaide.

Foolish girl!

Maid.

Children and fools —

*Enter*LIEBTRAUT.

Liebtraut.

Now, gracious lady, what do I deserve?

Adelaide.

Horns from your wife! — for judging from the present sample of your persuasive powers you have certainly endangered the honor of many a worthy family.

Liebtraut.

Not so, be assured, gracious lady.

Adelaide.

How did you contrive to bring him?

Liebtraut.

You know how they catch snipes, and why should I detail my little stratagems to you? — First, I pretended to have heard nothing, did not understand the reason of his behavior, and put him upon the disadvantage of telling me the whole story at length — then I saw the matter in quite a different light to what he did — could not find — could not see, and so forth — then I gossipped things great and small about Bamberg, and recalled to his memory certain old recollections; and when I had succeeded in occupying his imagination I knitted together many a broken association of ideas. He knew not what to say—felt a new attraction towards Bamberg—he would, and he would not. When I found him begin to waver, and saw him too much occupied with his own feelings to suspect my sincerity, I threw over his head a halter, woven of the three powerful cords, beauty, court-favor and flattery, and dragged him hither in triumph.

Adelaide.

What said you of me?

Liebtraut.

The simple truth—that you were in perplexity about your estates, and had hoped as he had so much influence with the emperor all would be satisfactorily settled.

Adelaide.

'Tis well.

Liebtraut.

The bishop will introduce him to you.

Adelaide.

I expect them. (*Exit*LIEBTRAUT.) And with such feelings have I seldom expected a visitor.

SCENE IV.—

The Spessart.
*Enter*SELBITZ, GOETZ*and*GEORGE*in the armor and dress of a trooper.*

Goetz.

So thou didst not find him, George?

George.

He had ridden to Bamberg the day before with Liebtraut and two servants.

Goetz.

I cannot understand what this means.

Selbitz.

I see it well—your reconciliation was almost too speedy to be lasting—Liebtraut is a cunning fellow, and has no doubt inveigled him over.
Goetz.
Think'st thou he will become a traitor?
Selbitz.
The first step is taken.
Goetz.
I will never believe it. Who knows what he may have to do at court—his affairs are still unarranged. Let us hope for the best.
Selbitz.
Would to Heaven he may deserve of your good opinion, and may act for the best!
Goetz.
A thought strikes me!—We will disguise George in the spoils of the Bamberg trooper, and furnish him with the password—he may then ride to Bamberg, and see how matters stand.
George.
I have long wished to do so.
Goetz.
It is thy first expedition. Be careful, boy; I should be sorry if ill befell thee.
George.
Never fear. I care not how many of them crawl about me; I think no more of them than of rats and mice.
[*Exeunt.*

SCENE V.—

*The*BISHOP'S*Palace. His Cabinet.*
*The*BISHOP*and*WEISLINGEN.
Bishop.
Then thou wilt stay no longer?
Weislingen.
You would not have me break my oath.

Bishop.
I could have wished thou hadst not sworn it. What evil spirit possessed thee? Could I not have procured thy release without that? Is my influence so small in the imperial court?

Weislingen.
The thing is done — excuse it as you can.

Bishop.
I cannot see that there was the least necessity for taking such a step. To renounce me? Were there not a thousand other ways of procuring thy freedom? Had we not his page? And would I not have given gold enough to boot, and thus satisfied Berlichingen? Our operations against him and his confederates could have gone on — But, alas! I do not reflect that I am talking to his friend, who has joined him against me, and can easily counterwork the mines he himself has dug.

Weislingen.
My gracious lord —

Bishop.
And yet — when I again look on thy face, again hear thy voice — it is impossible — impossible!

Weislingen.
Farewell, good my lord!

Bishop.
I give thee my blessing — formerly when we parted I was wont to say "Till we meet again!" Now Heaven grant we meet no more!

Weislingen.
Things may alter.

Bishop.
Perhaps I may live to see thee appear as an enemy before my walls, carrying havoc through the fertile plains which now owe their flourishing condition to thee.

Weislingen.
Never, my gracious lord!

Bishop.

You cannot say so. My temporal neighbors all have a grudge against me—but while thou wert mine— Go, Weislingen! I have no more to say. Thou hast undone much. Go—

Weislingen.

I know not what to answer.

[*Exit*BISHOP.

*Enter*FRANCIS.

Francis.

The Lady Adelaide expects you. She is not well, but she will not let you depart without bidding her adieu.

Weislingen.

Come.

Francis.

Do we go then for certain?

Weislingen.

This very night.

Francis.

I feel as if I were about to leave the world—

Weislingen.

I too, and as if besides I knew not whither to go.

SCENE VI.—

ADELAIDE'S*Apartment.*

ADELAIDE*and*WAITING-MAID.

Maid.

You are pale, gracious lady!

Adelaide.

I love him not, yet I wish him to stay—for I am fond of his company, though I should dislike him for my husband.

Maid.

Does your ladyship think he will go?

Adelaide.

He is even now bidding the bishop farewell.

Maid.

He has yet a severe struggle to undergo.

Adelaide.

What meanest thou?

Maid.

Why do you ask, gracious lady? The barbed hook is in his heart—ere he tear it away he must bleed to death.

Enter WEISLINGEN.

Weislingen.

You are not well, gracious lady?

Adelaide.

That must be indifferent to you—you leave us, leave us forever: what matters it to you whether we live or die?

Weislingen.

You do me injustice.

Adelaide.

I judge you as you appear.

Weislingen.

Appearances are deceitful.

Adelaide.

Then you are a chameleon.

Weislingen.

Could you but see my heart—

Adelaide.

I should see fine things there.

Weislingen.

Undoubtedly!—You would find your own image—

Adelaide.

Thrust into some dark corner with the pictures of defunct ancestors! I beseech you, Weislingen, consider with whom you speak—false words are of value only when they serve to veil our actions—a discovered masquerader plays a pitiful part. You do not disown your deeds, yet your words belie them; what are we to think of you?

Weislingen.

What you will—I am so agonized at reflecting on what I am, that I little reck for what I am taken.

Adelaide.

You came to say farewell.

Weislingen.

Permit me to kiss your hand, and I will say adieu!— You remind me—I did not think—but I am troublesome—

Adelaide.

You misinterpret me. Since you will depart, I only wished to assist your resolution.

Weislingen.

Oh, say rather, I must!—were I not compelled by my knightly word—my solemn engagement—

Adelaide.

Go to! Talk of that to maidens who read the tale of Theuerdanck, and wish that they had such a husband.— Knightly word!—Nonsense!

Weislingen.

You do not think so?

Adelaide.

On my honor, you are dissembling. What have you promised? and to whom? You have pledged your alliance to a traitor to the emperor, at the very moment when he incurred the ban of the empire by taking you prisoner. Such an agreement is no more binding than an extorted, unjust oath. And do not our laws release you from such oaths? Go, tell that to children, who believe in Rübezahl. There is something behind all this.— To become an enemy of the empire—a disturber of public happiness and tranquillity, an enemy of the emperor, the associate of a robber!—Thou, Weislingen, with thy gentle soul!

Weislingen.

Did you but know him!

Adelaide.

I would deal justly with Goetz. He has a lofty indomitable spirit, and woe to thee, therefore, Weislingen. Go, and persuade thyself thou art his companion. Go, and receive his commands. Thou art courteous, gentle—

Weislingen.

And he too.
Adelaide.
But thou art yielding, and he is stubborn. Imperceptibly will he draw thee on. Thou wilt become the slave of a baron; thou that mightest command princes!—Yet it is cruel to make you discontented with your future position.
Weislingen.
Did you but know what kindness he showed me.
Adelaide.
Kindness!—Do you make such a merit of that? It was his duty. And what would you have lost had he acted otherwise? I would rather he had done so. An overbearing man like—
Weislingen.
You speak of your enemy.
Adelaide.
I speak for your freedom; yet I know not why I should take so much interest in it. Farewell!
Weislingen.
Permit me, but a moment.
[*Takes her hand. A pause.*
Adelaide.
Have you aught to say?
Weislingen.
I must hence.
Adelaide.
Then go.
Weislingen.
Gracious lady, I cannot.
Adelaide.
You must.
Weislingen.
And is this your parting look?
Adelaide.
Go, I am unwell, very inopportunely.
Weislingen.
Look not on me thus!

Adelaide.
Wilt thou be our enemy, and yet have us smile upon thee? Go!
Weislingen.
Adelaide!
Adelaide.
I hate thee!
*Enter*FRANCIS.
Francis.
Noble sir, the bishop inquires for you.
Adelaide.
Go! go!
Francis.
He begs you to come instantly.
Adelaide.
Go! go!
Weislingen.
I do not say adieu: I shall see you again.
[*Exeunt*WEISLINGEN*and*FRANCIS.
Adelaide.
Thou wilt see me again? We must provide for that. Margaret, when he comes, refuse him admittance. Say I am ill, have a headache, am asleep, anything. If this does not detain him, nothing will.
[*Exeunt.*

SCENE VII. —

An Ante-room.

WEISLINGEN*and*FRANCIS.
Weislingen.
She will not see me!
Francis.
Night draws on; shall we saddle?
Weislingen.

She will not see me!
Francis.
Shall I order the horses?
Weislingen.
It is too late; we stay here.
Francis.
God be praised.
[*Exit.*
Weislingen.
(*Alone.*) Thou stayest! Be on thy guard—the temptation is great. My horse started at the castle gate. My good angel stood before him, he knew the danger that awaited me. Yet it would be wrong to leave in confusion the various affairs entrusted to me by the bishop, without at least so arranging them that my successor may be able to continue where I left off. That I can do without breach of faith to Berlichingen, and when it is done no one shall detain me. Yet it would have been better that I had never come. But I will away—to-morrow—or next day:— 'tis decided!
[*Exit.*

SCENE VIII.—

The Spessart.
Enter GOETZ, SELBITZ *and* GEORGE.
Selbitz.
You see it has turned out as I prophesied.
Goetz.
No, no, no.
George.
I tell you the truth, believe me. I did as you commanded, took the dress and password of the Bamberg trooper, and escorted some peasants of the Lower Rhine, who paid my expenses for my convoy.
Selbitz.

In that disguise? It might have cost thee dear.

George.

So I begin to think, now that it's over. A trooper who thinks of danger beforehand will never do anything great. I got safely to Bamberg, and in the very first inn I heard them tell how the bishop and Weislingen were reconciled, and how Weislingen was to marry the widow of Von Walldorf.

Goetz.

Mere gossip!

George.

I saw him as he led her to table. She is lovely, by my faith, most lovely! We all bowed—she thanked us all. He nodded, and seemed highly pleased. They passed on, and everybody murmured, "What a handsome pair!"

Goetz.

That may be.

George.

Listen further. The next day as he went to mass, I watched my opportunity; he was attended only by his squire; I stood at the steps, and whispered to him as he passed, "A few words from your friend Berlichingen." He started—I marked the confession of guilt in his face. He had scarcely the heart to look at me—me, a poor trooper's boy!

Selbitz.

His evil conscience degrades him more than thy condition does thee.

George.

"Art thou of Bamberg?" said he. "The Knight of Berlichingen greets you," said I, "and I am to inquire—" "Come to my apartment to-morrow morning," quoth he, "and we will speak further."

Goetz.

And you went?

George.

Yes, certainly, I went, and waited in his ante-chamber a long, long time—and his pages, in their silken doublets, stared at me from head to foot. Stare on, thought I. At length I was admitted. He seemed angry. But what cared I? I gave my message. He began blustering like a coward who wants to look brave. He wondered that you should take him to task through a trooper's boy. That angered me. "There are but two sorts of people," said I, "true men and scoundrels, and I serve Goetz of Berlichingen." Then he began to talk all manner of nonsense, which all tended to one point, namely, that you had hurried him into an agreement, that he owed you no allegiance, and would have nothing to do with you.

Goetz.

Hadst thou that from his own mouth?

George.

That, and yet more. He threatened me—

Goetz.

It is enough. He is lost forever. Faith and confidence, again have ye deceived me. Poor Maria! how am I to break this to you?

Selbitz.

I would rather lose my other leg than be such a rascal.

SCENE IX.—

Hall in the BISHOP'S *Palace at Bamberg.*
ADELAIDE *and* WEISLINGEN *discovered.*

Adelaide.

Time begins to hang insupportably heavy here. I dare not speak seriously, and I am ashamed to trifle with you. Ennui, thou art worse than a slow fever.

Weislingen.

Are you tired of me already?

Adelaide.

Not so much of you as of your society. I would you had gone when you wished, and that we had not detained you.

Weislingen.

Such is woman's favor! At first she fosters with maternal warmth our dearest hopes; and then, like an inconstant hen, she forsakes the nest, and abandons the infant brood to death and decay.

Adelaide.

Yes, you may rail at women. The reckless gambler tears and curses the harmless cards which have been the instruments of his loss. But let me tell you something about men. What are you that talk about fickleness? You that are seldom even what you would wish to be, never what you should be. Princes in holiday garb! the envy of the vulgar. Oh, what would a tailor's wife not give for a necklace of the pearls on the skirt of your robe, which you kick back contemptuously with your heels.

Weislingen.

You are severe.

Adelaide.

It is but the antistrophe to your song. Ere I knew you, Weislingen, I felt like the tailor's wife. Hundred-tongued rumor, to speak without metaphor, had so extolled you, in quack-doctor fashion, that I was tempted to wish—Oh, that I could but see this quintessence of manhood, this phœnix, Weislingen! My wish was granted.

Weislingen.

And the phœnix turned out a dunghill cock.

Adelaide.

No, Weislingen, I took an interest in you.

Weislingen.

So it appeared.

Adelaide.

So it *was*—for you really surpassed your reputation. The multitude prize only the reflection of worth. For my part, I do not care to scrutinize the character of those whom I esteem; so we lived on for some time. I felt there was a deficiency in you,

but knew not what I missed; at length my eyes were opened —
I saw instead of the energetic being who gave impulse to the
affairs of a kingdom, and was ever alive to the voice of fame —
who was wont to pile princely project on project, till, like the
mountains of the Titans, they reached the clouds — instead of
all this, I saw a man as querulous as a love-sick poet, as
melancholy as a slighted damsel, and more indolent than an
old bachelor. I first ascribed it to your misfortune which still
lay at your heart, and excused you as well as I could; but now
that it daily becomes worse, you must really forgive me if I
withdraw my favor from you. You possess it unjustly: I
bestowed it for life on a hero who cannot transfer it to you.

Weislingen.

Dismiss me, then.

Adelaide.

Not till all chance of recovery is lost. Solitude is fatal in your
distemper. Alas! poor man! you are as dejected as one whose
first love has proved false, and therefore I won't give you up.
Give me your hand, and pardon what affection has urged me
to say.

Weislingen.

Could'st thou but love me, could'st thou but return the fervor
of my passion with the least glow of sympathy. — Adelaide,
thy reproaches are most unjust. Could'st thou but guess the
hundredth part of my sufferings, thou would'st not have
tortured me so unmercifully with encouragement, indifference
and contempt. You smile. To be reconciled to myself after the
step I have taken must be the work of more than one day.
How can I plot against the man who has been so recently and
so vividly restored to my affection?

Adelaide.

Strange being! Can you love him whom you envy? It is like
sending provisions to an enemy.

Weislingen.

I well know that here there must be no dallying. He is aware
that I am again Weislingen; and he will watch his advantage

over us. Besides, Adelaide, we are not so sluggish as you think. Our troopers are reinforced and watchful, our schemes are proceeding, and the Diet of Augsburg will, I hope, soon bring them to a favorable issue.

Adelaide.

You go there?

Weislingen.

If I could carry a glimpse of hope with me.

[*Kisses her hand.*

Adelaide.

O ye infidels! Always signs and wonders required. Go, Weislingen, and accomplish the work! The interest of the bishop, yours and mine, are all so linked together, that were it only for policy's sake—

Weislingen.

You jest.

Adelaide.

I do not jest. The haughty duke has seized my property. Goetz will not be slow to ravage yours; and if we do not hold together, as our enemies do, and gain over the emperor to our side, we are lost.

Weislingen.

I fear nothing. Most of the princes think with us. The emperor needs assistance against the Turks, and it is therefore just that he should help us in his turn. What rapture for me to rescue your fortune from rapacious enemies; to crush the mutinous chivalry of Swabia; to restore peace to the bishopric, and then—

Adelaide.

One day brings on another, and fate is mistress of the future.

Weislingen.

But we must lend our endeavors.

Adelaide.

We do so.

Weislingen.

But seriously.

Adelaide.
Well, then, seriously. Do but go—
Weislingen.
Enchantress!
[*Exeunt.*

SCENE X—

An Inn.
The Bridal of a PEASANT.
[*The* BRIDE'S FATHER, BRIDE, BRIDEGROOM *and other Country-folks,* GOETZ OF BERLICHINGEN *and* HANS OF SELBITZ *all discovered at table.* TROOPERS *and* PEASANTS *attend.*
Goetz.
It was the best way thus to settle your lawsuit by a merry bridal.
Bride's Father.
Better than ever I could have dreamed of, noble sir—to spend my days in quiet with my neighbor, and have a daughter provided for to boot.
Bridegroom.
And I to get the bone of contention and a pretty wife into the bargain! Ay, the prettiest in the whole village. Would to Heaven you had consented sooner.
Goetz.
How long have you been at law?
Bride's Father.
About eight years. I would rather have the fever for twice that time than go through with it again from the beginning. For these periwigged gentry never give a decision till you tear it out of their very hearts; and, after all, what do you get for your pains? The devil fly away with the assessor Sapupi for a damned swarthy Italian!
Bridegroom.
Yes, he's a pretty fellow; I was before him twice.

Bride's Father.

And I thrice; and look ye, gentlemen, we got a judgment at last, which set forth that he was as much in the right as I, and I as much as he; so there we stood like a couple of fools, till a good Providence put it into my head to give him my daughter, and the ground besides.

Goetz.

(Drinks.) To your better understanding for the future.

Bride's Father.

With all my heart! But come what may, I'll never go to law again as long as I live. What a mint of money it costs! For every bow made to you by a procurator, you must come down with your dollars.

Selbitz.

But there are annual imperial visitations.

Bride's Father.

I have never heard of them. Many an extra dollar have they contrived to squeeze out of me. The expenses are horrible.

Goetz.

How mean you?

Bride's Father.

Why, look you, these gentlemen of the law are always holding out their hands. The assessor alone, God forgive him, eased me of eighteen golden guilders.

Bridegroom.

Who?

Bride's Father.

Why, who else but Sapupi?

Goetz.

That is infamous.

Bride's Father.

Yes, he asked twenty; and there I had to pay them in the great hall of his fine country-house. I thought my heart would burst with anguish. For look you, my lord, I am well enough off with my house and little farm, but how could I raise the ready cash? I stood there, God knows how it was with me. I had not a single farthing to carry me on my journey. At last I took courage and told him my case: when he saw I was desperate, he flung me back a couple of guilders, and sent me about my business.

Bridegroom.

Impossible! Sapupi?

Bride's Father.

Ay, he himself! — What do you stare at?

Bridegroom.

Devil take the rascal! He took fifteen guilders from me too?

Bride's Father.

The deuce he did!

Selbitz.

They call us robbers, Goetz!

Bride's Father.

Bribed on both sides!

That's why the judgment fell out so queer.

Oh, the scoundrel!

Goetz.

You must not let this pass unnoticed.

Bride's Father.

What can we do?

Goetz.

Why — go to Spire where there is an imperial visitation: make your complaint; they must inquire into it, and help you to your own again.

Bridegroom.

Does your honor think we shall succeed?

Goetz.

If I might take him in hand, I could promise it you.

Selbitz.

The sum is worth an attempt.

Goetz.

Ay; many a day have I ridden out for the fourth part of it.

Bride's Father.

(*To*BRIDEGROOM.) What think'st thou?

Bridegroom.

We'll try, come what may.

Enter GEORGE.

George.

The Nurembergers have set out.

Goetz.

Whereabouts are they?

George.

If we ride off quietly we shall just catch them in the wood betwixt Berheim and Mühlbach.

Selbitz.

Excellent!

Goetz.

Well, my children, God bless you, and help every man to his own!

Bride's Father.

Thanks, gallant sir! Will you not stay to supper?

Goetz.

I cannot. Adieu!

[*Exeunt* GOETZ, SELBITZ *and* TROOPERS

ACT III.

SCENE I. —

A Garden at Augsburg.
Enter two MERCHANTS *of Nuremberg.*

First Merchant.
We'll stand here, for the emperor must pass this way. He is just coming up the long avenue.

Second Merchant.
Who is that with him?

First Merchant.
Adelbert of Weislingen.

Second Merchant.
The bishop's friend. That's lucky!

First Merchant.
We'll throw ourselves at his feet.

Second Merchant.
See! they come.

Enter the EMPEROR *and* WEISLINGEN.

First Merchant.
He looks displeased.

Emperor.
I am disheartened, Weislingen. When I review my past life, I am ready to despair. So many half—ay, and wholly ruined undertakings—and all because the pettiest feudatory of the empire thinks more of gratifying his own whims than of seconding my endeavors.

[*The* MERCHANTS *throw themselves at his feet.*

First Merchant.

Most mighty! Most gracious!

Emperor.

Who are ye? What seek ye?

First Merchant.

Poor merchants of Nuremberg, your majesty's devoted servants, who implore your aid. Goetz von Berlichingen and Hans von Selbitz fell upon thirty of us as we journeyed from the fair of Frankfort, under an escort from Bamberg; they overpowered and plundered us. We implore your imperial assistance to obtain redress, else we are all ruined men, and shall be compelled to beg our bread.

Emperor.

Good heavens! What is this? The one has but one hand, the other but one leg; if they both had two hands and two legs what would you do then?

First Merchant.

We most humbly beseech your majesty to cast a look of compassion upon our unfortunate condition.

Emperor.

How is this?—If a merchant loses a bag of pepper, all Germany is to rise in arms; but when business is to be done, in which the imperial majesty and the empire are interested, should it concern dukedoms, principalities, or kingdoms, there is no bringing you together.

Weislingen.

You come at an unseasonable time. Go, and stay at Augsburg for a few days.

Merchants.

We make our most humble obeisance.

[*Exeunt*MERCHANTS.

Emperor.

Again new disturbances; they multiply like the hydra's heads!

Weislingen.

And can only be extirpated with fire and sword.

Emperor.

Do you think so?

Weislingen.

Nothing seems to me more advisable, could your majesty and the princes but accommodate your other unimportant disputes. It is not the body of the state that complains of this malady — Franconia and Swabia alone glow with the embers of civil discord; and even there many of the nobles and free barons long for quiet. Could we but crush Sickingen, Selbitz — and — and — and Berlichingen, the others would fall asunder; for it is the spirit of these knights which quickens the turbulent multitude.

Emperor.

Fain would I spare them; they are noble and hardy. Should I be engaged in war, they would follow me to the field.

Weislingen.

It is to be wished they had at all times known their duty; moreover it would be dangerous to reward their mutinous bravery by offices of trust. For it is exactly this imperial mercy and forgiveness which they have hitherto so grievously abused, and upon which the hope and confidence of their league rest, and this spirit cannot be quelled till we have wholly destroyed their power in the eyes of the world, and taken from them all hope of ever recovering their lost influence.

Emperor.

You advise severe measures, then?

Weislingen.

I see no other means of quelling the spirit of insurrection which has seized upon whole provinces. Do we not already hear the bitterest complaints from the nobles, that their vassals and serfs rebel against them, question their authority, and threaten to curtail their hereditary prerogatives? A proceeding which would involve the most fearful consequences.

Emperor.

This were a fair occasion for proceeding against Berlichingen and Selbitz; but I will not have them personally injured. Could they be taken prisoners, they should swear to renounce their

feuds, and to remain in their own castles and territories upon their knightly parole. At the next session of the Diet we will propose this plan.
Weislingen.
A general exclamation of joyful assent will spare your majesty the trouble of particular detail.
[*Exeunt.*

SCENE II. —

Jaxthausen.
*Enter*GOETZ*and*FRANZ VON SICKINGEN.
Sickingen.
Yes, my friend, I come to beg the heart and hand of your noble sister.
Goetz.
I would you had come sooner. Weislingen, during his imprisonment, obtained her affections, proposed for her, and I gave my consent. I let the bird loose, and he now despises the benevolent hand that fed him in his distress. He flutters about to seek his food, God knows upon what hedge.
Sickingen.
Is this so?
Goetz.
Even as I tell you.
Sickingen.
He has broken a double bond. 'Tis well for you that you were not more closely allied with the traitor.
Goetz.
The poor maiden passes her life in lamentation and prayer.
Sickingen.
I will comfort her.
Goetz.
What! Could you make up your mind to marry a forsaken—
Sickingen.

It is to the honor of you both to have been deceived by him. Should the poor girl be caged in a cloister because the first man who gained her love proved a villain? Not so; I insist on it. She shall be mistress of my castles!

Goetz.

I tell you he was not indifferent to her.

Sickingen.

Do you think I cannot efface the recollection of such a wretch? Let us go to her.

[*Exeunt.*

SCENE III. —

The Camp of the Party sent to execute the Imperial Mandate.
Imperial CAPTAIN *and* OFFICERS *discovered.*

Captain.

We must be cautious, and spare our people as much as possible. Besides, we have strict orders to overpower and take him alive. It will be difficult to obey; for who will engage with him hand to hand?

First Officer.

'Tis true. And he will fight like a wild boar. Besides, he has never in his whole life injured any of us, so each will be glad to leave to the other the honor of risking life and limb to please the emperor.

Second Officer.

'Twere shame to us should we not take him. Had I him once by the ears, he should not easily escape.

First Officer.

Don't seize him with your teeth, however, he might chance to run away with your jaw-bone. My good young sir, such men are not taken like a runaway thief.

Second Officer.

We shall see.

Captain.

By this time he must have had our summons. We must not delay. I mean to despatch a troop to watch his motions.

Second Officer.

Let me lead it.

Captain.

You are unacquainted with the country.

Second Officer.

I have a servant who was born and bred here.

Captain.

That will do.

[*Exeunt.*

SCENE IV. —

Jaxthausen.

Sickingen.

(*Alone.*) All goes as I wish! She was somewhat startled at my proposal, and looked at me from head to foot; I'll wager she was comparing me with her gallant. Thank Heaven I can stand the scrutiny! She answered little and confusedly. So much the better! Let it work for a time. A proposal of marriage does not come amiss after such a cruel disappointment.

Enter GOETZ.

Sickingen.

What news, brother?

Goetz.

They have laid me under the ban.

Sickingen.

How?

Goetz.

There, read the edifying epistle. The emperor has issued an edict against me, which gives my body for food to the beasts of the earth and the fowls of the air.

Sickingen.

They shall first furnish them with a dinner themselves. I am here in the very nick of time.

Goetz.

No, Sickingen, you must leave me. Your great undertakings might be ruined should you become the enemy of the emperor at so unseasonable a time. Besides, you can be of more use to me by remaining neutral. The worst that can happen is my being made prisoner; and then your good word with the emperor, who esteems you, may rescue me from the misfortune into which your untimely assistance would irremediably plunge us both. To what purpose should you do otherwise? These troops are marching against me; and if they knew we were united, their numbers would only be increased, and our position would consequently be no better. The emperor is at the fountain-head; and I should be utterly ruined were it as easy to inspire soldiers with courage as to collect them into a body.

Sickingen.

But I can privately reinforce you with a score of troopers.

Goetz.

Good. I have already sent George to Selbitz, and to my people in the neighborhood. My dear brother, when my forces are collected, they will be such a troop as few princes can bring together.

Sickingen.

It will be small against the multitude.

Goetz.

One wolf is too many for a whole flock of sheep.

Sickingen.

But if they have a good shepherd?

Goetz.

Never fear! They are all hirelings; and then even the best knight can do but little if he cannot act as he pleases. It happened once that, to oblige the palsgrave, I went to serve against Conrad Schotten: they then presented me with a paper of instructions from the chancery, which set forth — Thus and thus must you proceed. I threw down the paper before the magistrates, and told them I could not act according to it; that something might happen unprovided for in my instructions, and that I must use my own eyes and judge what was best to be done.

Sickingen.

Good luck, brother! I will hence, and send thee what men I can collect in haste.

Goetz.

Come first to the women. I left them together. I would you had her consent before you depart! Then send me the troopers, and come back in private to carry away my Maria; for my castle, I fear, will shortly be no abode for women.

Sickingen.

We will hope for the best.

[*Exeunt.*

SCENE V. —

Bamberg. ADELAIDE'S *Chamber.*

ADELAIDE *and* FRANCIS.

Adelaide.

They have already set out to enforce the ban against both?

Francis.

Yes; and my master has the happiness of marching against your enemies. I would gladly have gone also, however rejoiced I always am at being despatched to you. But I will away instantly, and soon return with good news; my master has allowed me to do so.

Adelaide.

How is he?
Francis.
He is well, and commanded me to kiss your hand.
Adelaide.
There! — Thy lips glow.
Francis.
(Aside, pressing his breast.) Here glows something yet more fiery. *(Aloud.)* Gracious lady, your servants are the most fortunate of beings!
Adelaide.
Who goes against Berlichingen?
Francis.
The Baron von Sirau. Farewell! Dearest, most gracious lady, I must away. Forget me not!
Adelaide.
Thou must first take some rest and refreshment.
Francis.
I need none, for I have seen you! I am neither weary nor hungry.
Adelaide.
I know thy fidelity.
Francis.
Ah, gracious lady!
Adelaide.
You can never hold out; you *must* repose and refresh yourself.
Francis.
You are too kind to a poor youth.
[*Exit.*
Adelaide.
The tears stood in his eyes. I love him from my heart. Never did man attach himself to me with such warmth of affection.
[*Exit.*

SCENE VI. —

Jaxthausen.
GOETZ *and* GEORGE.
George.
He wants to speak with you in person. I do not know him — he is a tall, well-made man, with keen dark eyes.
Goetz.
Admit him.
[*Exit* GEORGE.
Enter LERSE.
Goetz.
God save you! What bring you?
Lerse.
Myself: not much, but such as it is, it is at your service.
Goetz.
You are welcome, doubly welcome! A brave man, and at a time when, far from expecting new friends. I was in hourly fear of losing the old. Your name?
Lerse.
Franz Lerse.
Goetz.
I thank you, Franz, for making me acquainted with a brave man!
Lerse.
I made you acquainted with me once before, but then you did not thank me for my pains.
Goetz.
I have no recollection of you.
Lerse.
I should be sorry if you had. Do you recollect when, to please the palsgrave, you rode against Conrad Schotten, and went through Hassfurt on an All-hallow eve?
Goetz.
I remember it well.
Lerse.

And twenty-five troopers encountered you in a village by the way?

Goetz.

Exactly. I at first took them for only twelve. I divided my party, which amounted to but sixteen, and halted in the village behind the barn, intending to let them ride by. Then I thought of falling upon them in the rear, as I had concerted with the other troop.

Lerse.

We saw you, however, and stationed ourselves on a height above the village. You drew up beneath the hill and halted. When we perceived that you did not intend to come up to us we rode down to you.

Goetz.

And then I saw for the first time that I had thrust my hand into the fire. Five-and-twenty against eight is no jesting business. Everard Truchsess killed one of my followers, for which I knocked him off his horse. Had they all behaved like him and one other trooper, it would have been all over with me and my little band.

Lerse.

And that trooper —

Goetz.

Was as gallant a fellow as I ever saw. He attacked me fiercely; and when I thought I had given him enough and was engaged elsewhere, he was upon me again, and laid on like a fury: he cut quite through my armor, and wounded me in the arm.

Lerse.

Have you forgiven him?

Goetz.

He pleased me only too well.

Lerse.

I hope then you have cause to be contented with me, since the proof of my valor was on your own person.

Goetz.

Art thou he? O welcome! welcome! Canst thou boast, Maximilian, that amongst thy followers thou hast gained one after this fashion?

Lerse.

I wonder you did not sooner hit upon me.

Goetz.

How could I think that the man would engage in my service who did his best to overpower me?

Lerse.

Even so, my lord. From my youth upwards I have served as a trooper, and have had a tussle with many a knight. I was overjoyed when we met you; for I had heard of your prowess, and wished to know you. You saw I gave way, and that it was not from cowardice, for I returned to the charge. In short, I learned to know you, and from that hour I resolved to enter your service.

Goetz.

How long wilt thou engage with me?

Lerse.

For a year, without pay.

Goetz.

No; thou shalt have as the others; nay more, as befits him who gave me so much work at Remlin.

Enter GEORGE.

George.

Hans of Selbitz greets you. To-morrow he will be here with fifty men.

Goetz.

'Tis well.

George.

There is a troop of Imperialists riding down the hill, doubtless to reconnoitre.

Goetz.

How many?

George.

About fifty.

Goetz.

Only fifty! Come, Lerse, we'll have a slash at them, so that when Selbitz comes he may find some work done to his hand.

Lerse.

'Twill be capital practice.

Goetz.

To horse!

[*Exeunt.*

SCENE VII. —

A Wood on the borders of a Morass.

*Two*IMPERIALIST TROOPERS*meeting*

First Imperialist.

What dost thou here?

Second Imperialist.

I have leave of absence for ten minutes. Ever since our quarters were beat up last night I have had such violent attacks that I can't sit on horseback for two minutes together.

First Imperialist.

Is the party far advanced?

Second Imperialist.

About three miles into the wood

First Imperialist.

Then why are you playing truant here?

Second Imperialist.

Prithee, betray me not. I am going to the next village to see if I cannot get some warm bandages to relieve my complaint. But whence comest thou?

First Imperialist.

I am bringing our officer some wine and meat from the nearest village.

Second Imperialist.

So, so! he stuffs himself under our very noses, and we must starve; a fine example!

First Imperialist.

Come back with me, rascal!

Second Imperialist.

Call me a fool, if I do! There are plenty in our troop who would gladly fast, to be as far away as I am.

[*Tramping of horses heard.*

First Imperialist.

Hear'st thou? — Horses!

Second Imperialist.

Oh dear! oh dear!

First Imperialist.

I'll get up into this tree.

Second Imperialist.

And I'll hide among the rushes.

[*They hide themselves.*

*Enter on horseback,*GOETZ. LERSE. GEORGE*and*TROOPERS,*all completely armed*

Goetz.

Away into the wood, by the ditch on the left, — then we have them in the rear.

[*They gallop off.*

First Imperialist.

(*Descending*) This is a bad business — Michael! — He answers not — Michael, they are gone! (*Goes towards the marsh.*) Alas, he is sunk! — Michael! — He hears me not: he is suffocated. — Poor coward, art thou done for? — We are slain. — Enemies! Enemies on all sides!

*Re-enter*GOETZ*and*GEORGE*on horseback.*

Goetz.

Yield thee, fellow, or thou diest!

Imperialist.

Spare my life!

Goetz.

Thy sword!—George, lead him to the other prisoners whom Lerse is guarding yonder in the wood.—I must pursue their fugitive leader.
[*Exit.*

Imperialist.
What has become of the knight, our officer?

George.
My master struck him head over heels from his horse, so that his plume stuck in the mire. His troopers got him up, and off they were as if the devil were behind them.
[*Exeunt.*

SCENE VIII.—

*Camp of the*IMPERIALISTS.
CAPTAIN*and*FIRST OFFICER.

First Officer.
They fly from afar towards the camp.

Captain.
He is most likely hard at their heels. Draw out fifty as far as the mill; if he follows up the pursuit too far you may perhaps entrap him.
[*Exit*OFFICER.
*The*SECOND OFFICER*is borne in.*

Captain.
How now, my young sir—have you got a cracked headpiece?

Officer.
A plague upon you! The stoutest helmet went to shivers like glass. The demon!—he ran upon me as if he would strike me into the earth!

Captain.
Thank God that you have escaped with your life.

Officer.
There is little left to be thankful for; two of my ribs are broken—where's the surgeon?

[*He is carried off.*

SCENE IX. —

Jaxthausen.
Enter GOETZ *and* SELBITZ.
Goetz.
And what say you to the ban, Selbitz?
Selbitz.
'Tis a trick of Weislingen's.
Goetz.
Do you think so?
Selbitz.
I do not think — I know it.
Goetz.
How so?
Selbitz.
He was at the Diet, I tell thee, and near the emperor's person.
Goetz.
Well then, we shall frustrate another of his schemes.
Selbitz.
I hope so.
Goetz.
We will away, and course these hares.

SCENE X. —

The Imperial Camp.
CAPTAIN. OFFICERS *and* FOLLOWERS.
Captain.
We shall gain nothing at this work, sirs! He beats one troop after another; and whoever escapes death or captivity would rather fly to Turkey than return to the camp. Thus our force diminishes daily. We must attack him once for all, and in

earnest. I will go myself, and he shall find with whom he has to deal.

Officer.

We are all content; but he is so well acquainted with the country, and knows every path and ravine so thoroughly, that he will be as difficult to find as a rat in a barn.

Captain.

I warrant you we'll ferret him out. On towards Jaxthausen! Whether he like it or not, he must come to defend his castle.

Officer.

Shall our whole force march?

Captain.

Yes, certainly—do you know that a hundred of us are melted away already?

Officer.

Then let us away with speed, before the whole snowball dissolves; for this is warm work, and we stand here like butter in the sunshine.

[*Exeunt — a march sounded.*

SCENE XI. —

Mountains and a Wood.

GOETZ, SELBITZ*and*TROOPERS.

Goetz.

They are coming in full force. It was high time that Sickingen's troopers joined us.

Selbitz.

We will divide our party—I will take the left hand by the hill.

Goetz.

Good—and do thou, Lerse, lead fifty men straight through the wood on the right. They are coming across the heath—I will draw up opposite to them. George, stay by me—when you see

them attack me, then fall upon their flank: we'll beat the knaves into a mummy — they little think we can face them.
[*Exeunt.*

SCENE XII. —

A Heath — on one side an Eminence, with a ruined Tower, on the other the Forest.
Enter marching, the CAPTAIN OF THE IMPERIALISTS *with* OFFICERS *and his* SQUADRON. *Drums and standards.*

Captain.
He halts upon the heath! that's too impudent. He shall smart for it — what! not fear the torrent that threatens to overwhelm him!

Officer.
I had rather you did not head the troops; he looks as if he meant to plant the first that comes upon him in the mire with his head downmost. Prithee, ride in the rear.

Captain.
Not so.

Officer.
I entreat you. You are the knot which unites this bundle of hazel-twigs; loose it, and he will break them separately like so many reeds.

Captain.
Sound, trumpeter — and let us blow him to hell!
[*A charge sounded. Exeunt in full career.*
SELBITZ, *with his* TROOPERS, *comes from behind the hill, galloping.*

Selbitz.
Follow me! They shall wish that they could multiply their hands.
[*They gallop across the stage, et exeunt.*
Loud alarm — LERSE *and his party sally from the wood.*

Lerse.

Ho! to the rescue! Goetz is almost surrounded.—Gallant Selbitz, thou hast cut thy way—we will sow the heath with these thistle heads.

[Gallop off.
*A loud alarm, with shouting and firing for some minutes.*SELBITZ*is borne in wounded by two*TROOPERS.

Selbitz.

Leave me here, and hasten to Goetz.

First Trooper.

Let us stay, sir—you need our aid.

Selbitz.

Get one of you on the watchtower, and tell me how it goes.

First Trooper.

How shall I get up?

Second Trooper.

Mount upon my shoulders—you can then reach the ruined part, and thence scramble up to the opening.

*[FIRST TROOPER*gets up into the tower.*

First Trooper.

Alas, sir!

Selbitz.

What seest thou?

First Trooper.

Your troopers fly towards the hill.

Selbitz.

Rascally cowards! I would that they stood their ground, and I had a ball through my head! Ride, one of you, full speed! Curse and thunder them back to the field! Seest thou Goetz!

*[Exit*SECOND TROOPER.

Trooper.

I see his three black feathers floating in the midst of the wavy tumult.

Selbitz.

Swim, brave swimmer! I lie here.

Trooper.

A white plume — whose is that?

Selbitz.

The captain's.

Trooper.

Goetz gallops upon him — crash! Down he goes!

Selbitz.

The captain?

Trooper.

Yes, sir.

Selbitz.

Hurrah! hurrah!

Trooper.

Alas! alas! I see Goetz no more.

Selbitz.

Then die, Selbitz!

Trooper.

A dreadful tumult where he stood — George's blue plume vanishes too.

Selbitz.

Come down! Dost thou not see Lerse?

Trooper.

No. Everything is in confusion.

Selbitz.

No more. Come down. — How do Sickingen's men bear themselves?

Trooper.

Well — one of them flies to the wood — another — another — a whole troop. Goetz is lost!

Selbitz.

Come down.

Trooper.

I cannot. — Hurrah! hurrah! I see Goetz, I see George.

Selbitz.

On horseback?

Trooper.

Ay, ay, high on horseback! Victory! victory! — they fly.

Selbitz.

The Imperialists?

Trooper.

Yes, standard and all, Goetz behind them. They disperse,— Goetz reaches the ensign—he seizes the standard; he halts. A handful of men rally round him. My comrade reaches him— they come this way.

*Enter*GOETZ, GEORGE, LERSE*and*TROOPERS,*on horseback.*

Selbitz.

Joy to thee, Goetz! Victory! victory!

Goetz.

(Dismounting.) Dearly, dearly bought. Thou art wounded, Selbitz!

Selbitz.

But thou dost live and hast conquered! I have done little; and my dogs of troopers! How hast thou come off?

Goetz.

For the present, well! And here I thank George, and thee, Lerse, for my life. I unhorsed the captain, they stabbed my horse, and pressed me hard. George cut his way to me, and sprang off his horse. I threw myself like lightning upon it, and he appeared suddenly like a thunderbolt upon another, How camest thou by thy steed?

George.

A fellow struck at you from behind: as he raised his cuirass in the act, I stabbed him with my dagger. Down he came; and so I rid you of an enemy, and helped myself to a horse.

Goetz.

There we held together till Francis here came to our help; and thereupon we mowed our way out.

ARTIST: A. WAGNER.
GÖTZ VON BERLICHINGEN. ACT III.
GOTZ VON BERLICHINGEN AND SELBITZ.

Lerse.

The hounds whom I led were to have mowed their way in, till our scythes met, but they fled like Imperialists.

Goetz.

Friend and foe all fled, except this little band who protected my rear. I had enough to do with the fellows in front, but the fall of their captain dismayed them; they wavered, and fled. I have their banner, and a few prisoners.

Selbitz.

The captain has escaped you?

Goetz.

They rescued him in the scuffle. Come, lads, come, Selbitz — Make a litter of lances and boughs: thou canst not mount a horse, come to my castle. They are scattered, but we are very few; and I know not what troops they may have in reserve. I will be your host, my friends. Wine will taste well after such an action.

[*Exeunt, carrying* SELBITZ.

SCENE XIII. —

The Camp.

The CAPTAIN *and* IMPERIALISTS.

Captain.

I could kill you all with my own hand. — What! to turn tail! He had not a handful of men left. To give way before one man! No one will believe it but those who wish to make a jest of us. Ride round the country, you, and you, and you: collect our scattered soldiers, or cut them down wherever you find them. We must grind these notches out of our blades, even should we spoil our swords in the operation.

[*Exeunt.*

SCENE XIV. —

Jaxthausen.
GOETZ, LERSE*and*GEORGE.
Goetz.
We must not lose a moment. My poor fellows, I dare allow you no rest. Gallop round and strive to enlist troopers, appoint them to assemble at Weilern, where they will be most secure. Should we delay a moment, they will be before the castle. — (*Exeunt*LERSE*and*GEORGE) — I must send out a scout. This begins to grow warm. — If we had but brave foemen to deal with! But these fellows are only formidable through their number.
[*Exit.*
*Enter*SICKINGEN*and*MARIA.
Maria.
I beseech thee, dear Sickingen, do not leave my brother! His horsemen, your own, and those of Selbitz, all are scattered; he is alone. Selbitz has been carried home to his castle wounded. I fear the worst.
Sickingen.
Be comforted, I will not leave him.
*Enter*GOETZ.
Goetz.
Come to the chapel; the priest waits; in a few minutes you shall be united.
Sickingen.
Let me remain with you.
Goetz.
You must come now to the chapel.
Sickingen.
Willingly! — and then —
Goetz.
Then you go your way.
Sickingen.
Goetz!

Goetz.

Will you not to the chapel?

Sickingen.

Come, come!

[*Exeunt.*

SCENE XV. —

Camp.

CAPTAIN*and*OFFICERS.

Captain.

How many are we in all?

Officer.

A hundred and fifty —

Captain.

Out of four hundred. — That is bad. Set out for Jaxthausen at once, before he collects his forces and attacks us on the way.

SCENE XVI. —

Jaxthausen.

GOETZ, ELIZABETH, MARIA*and*SICKINGEN.

Goetz.

God bless you, give you happy days, and keep those for your children which he denies to you!

Elizabeth.

And may they be virtuous as you — then let come what will.

Sickingen.

I thank you. — And you, my Maria! As I led you to the altar, so shall you lead me to happiness.

Maria.

Our pilgrimage will be together towards that distant and promised land.

Goetz.

A prosperous journey.

Maria.

That was not what I meant. — We do not leave you.

Goetz.

You must, sister.

Maria.

You are very harsh, brother.

Goetz.

And you more affectionate than prudent.

*Enter*GEORGE.

George.

*(Aside to*GOETZ.*)* I can collect no troopers. One was inclined to come, but he changed his mind and refused.

Goetz.

*(To*GEORGE.*)* 'Tis well, George. Fortune begins to look coldly on me. I foreboded it, however. *(Aloud.)* Sickingen, I entreat you, depart this very evening. Persuade Maria. — You are her husband — let her feel it. — When women come across our undertakings, our enemies are more secure in the open field, than they would else be in their castles.

*Enter a*TROOPER.

Trooper.

*(Aside to*GOETZ.*)* The Imperial squadron is in full and rapid march hither.

Goetz.

I have roused them with stripes of the rod! How many are they?

Trooper.

About two hundred. — They can scarcely be six miles from us.

Goetz.

Have they passed the river yet?

Trooper.

No, my lord.

Goetz.

Had I but fifty men, they should not cross it. Hast thou seen Lerse?

Trooper.

No, my lord.

Goetz.

Tell all to hold themselves ready. — We must part, dear friends. Weep on, my gentle Maria; many a moment of happiness is yet in store for thee. It is better thou should'st weep on thy wedding-day than that present joy should be the forerunner of future misery. — Farewell, Maria! — Farewell, brother!

Maria.

I cannot leave you, sister. Dear brother, let us stay. Dost thou value my husband so little as to refuse his help in thy extremity?

Goetz.

Yes — it is gone far with me. Perhaps my fall is near. You are but beginning life, and should separate your lot from mine. I have ordered your horses to be saddled: you must away instantly.

Maria.

Brother! brother!

Elizabeth.

(*To*SICKINGEN.) Yield to his wishes. Speak to her.

Sickingen.

Dear Maria! we must go.

Maria.

Thou too? My heart will break!

Goetz.

Then stay. In a few hours my castle will be surrounded.

Maria.

(*Weeping bitterly.*) Alas! alas!

Goetz.

We will defend ourselves as long as we can.

Maria.

Mother of God, have mercy upon us!

Goetz.

And at last we must die or surrender. Thy tears will then have involved thy noble husband in the same misfortune with me.

Maria.

Thou torturest me!

Goetz.

Remain! remain! We shall be taken together! Sickingen, thou wilt fall into the pit with me, out of which I had hoped thou should'st have helped me.

Maria.

We will away. — Sister — sister!

Goetz.

Place her in safety, and then think of me.

Sickingen.

Never will I repose a night by her side till I know thou art out of danger.

Goetz.

Sister! dear sister!

[*Kisses her.*

Sickingen.

Away! away!

Goetz.

Yet one moment! I shall see you again. Be comforted, we shall meet again. (*Exeunt*SICKINGEN*and*MARIA.) I urged her to depart — yet when she leaves me what would I not give to detain her! Elizabeth, thou stayest with me.

Elizabeth.

Till death!

[*Exit.*

Goetz.

Whom God loves, to him may He give such a wife.

*Enter*GEORGE.

George.

They are near! I saw them from the tower. The sun is rising, and I perceived their lances glitter. I cared no more for them than a cat would for a whole army of mice. 'Tis true *we* play the mice at present.

Goetz.

Look to the fastenings of the gates; barricade them with beams and stones. (*Exit*GEORGE.) We'll exercise their patience, and they may chew away their valor in biting their nails. (*A trumpet from without.*GOETZ*goes to the window.*) Aha! Here comes a red-coated rascal to ask me whether I will be a scoundrel! What says he? (*The voice of the*HERALD*is heard indistinctly, as from a distance.*GOETZ*mutters to himself.*) A rope for thy throat! (*Voice again.*) "Offended majesty!" —Some priest has drawn up that proclamation. (*Voice concludes, and*GOETZ*answers from the window.*) Surrender—surrender at discretion. With whom speak you? Am I a robber? Tell your captain, that for the emperor I entertain, as I have ever done, all due respect; but as for him, he may—
[*Shuts the window with violence.*

SCENE XVII. —

The kitchen.
ELIZABETH*preparing food. Enter*GOETZ.
Goetz.
You have hard work, my poor wife!
Elizabeth.
Would it might last! But you can hardly hold out long.
Goetz.
We have not had time to provide ourselves.
Elizabeth.
And so many people as you have been wont to entertain. The wine is well-nigh finished.
Goetz.
If we can but hold out a certain time, they must propose a capitulation. We are doing them some damage, I promise you. They shoot the whole day, and only wound our walls and break our windows. Lerse is a gallant fellow. He slips about with his gun: if a rogue comes too nigh—Pop! there he lies!
[*Firing.*

Enter TROOPER.

Trooper.

We want live coals, gracious lady!

Goetz.

For what?

Trooper.

Our bullets are spent; we must cast some new ones.

Goetz.

How goes it with the powder?

Trooper.

There is as yet no want: we save our fire.

[*Firing at intervals. Exeunt* GOETZ *and* ELIZABETH.

Enter LERSE *with a bullet-mould. Servants with coals.*

Lerse.

Set them down, and then go and see for lead about the house; meanwhile I will make shift with this. (*Goes to the window, and takes out the leaden frames.*) Everything must be turned to account. So it is in this world—no one knows what a thing may come to: the glazier who made these frames little thought that the lead here was to give one of his grandsons his last headache; and the father that begot me little knew whether the fowls of heaven or the worms of the earth would pick my bones.

Enter GEORGE *with a leaden spout.*

George.

Here's lead for thee! If you hit with only half of it, not one will return to tell his majesty. "Thy servants have sped ill!"

Lerse.

(*Cutting it down.*) A famous piece!

George.

The rain must seek some other way. I'm not afraid of it—a brave trooper and a smart shower will always find their road.

[*They cast balls.*

Lerse.

Hold the ladle. *(Goes to the window.)* Yonder is a fellow creeping about with his rifle; he thinks our fire is spent. He shall have a bullet warm from the pan.

[*He loads his rifle.*

George.

(Puts down the mould.) Let me see.

Lerse.

(Fires.) There lies the game!

George.

He fired at me as I stepped out on the roof to get the lead. He killed a pigeon that sat near me; it fell into the spout. I thanked him for my dinner, and went back with the double booty.

[*They cast balls.*

Lerse.

Now let us load, and go through the castle to earn our dinner.

*Enter*GOETZ.

Goetz.

Stay, Lerse, I must speak with thee. I will not keep thee, George, from the sport.

[*Exit*GEORGE.

Goetz.

They offer terms.

Lerse.

I will go and hear what they have to say.

Goetz.

They will require me to enter myself into ward in some town on my knightly parole.

Lerse.

That won't do. Suppose they allow us free liberty of departure? for we can expect no relief from Sickingen. We will bury all the valuables where no divining-rod shall find them; leave them the bare walls, and come out with flying colors.

Goetz.

They will not permit us.

Lerse.

It is worth the asking. We will demand a safe-conduct, and I will sally out.

SCENE XVIII.—

A Hall.

GOETZ, ELIZABETH, GEORGE*and*TROOPERS*at table.*

Goetz.

Danger unites us, my friends! Be of good cheer; don't forget the bottle! The flask is empty. Come, another, dear wife! (ELIZABETH*shakes her head.*) Is there no more?

Elizabeth.

(*Aside.*) Only one, which I have set apart for you.

Goetz.

Not so, my love! Bring it out; they need strengthening more than I, for it is my quarrel.

Elizabeth.

Fetch it from the cupboard.

Goetz.

It is the last, and I feel as if we need not spare it. It is long since I have been so merry. (*They fill.*) To the health of the emperor!

All.

Long live the emperor!

Goetz.

Be it our last word when we die! I love him, for our fate is similar; but I am happier than he. To please the princes, he must direct his imperial squadrons against mice, while the rats gnaw his possessions.—I know he often wishes himself dead, rather than to be any longer the soul of such a crippled body. (*They fill.*) It will just go once more round. And when our blood runs low, like this flask—when we pour out its last ebbing drop (*empties the wine drop by drop into his goblet*)—what then shall be our cry?

George.

Freedom forever!

Goetz.

Freedom forever!

All.

Freedom forever!

Goetz.

And if that survive us we can die happy; for our spirits shall see our children's children and their emperor happy! Did the servants of princes show the same filial attachment to their masters as you to me—did their masters serve the emperor as I would serve him—

George.

Things would be widely different.

Goetz.

Not so much so as it would appear. Have I not known worthy men among the princes? And can the race be extinct? Men, happy in their own minds and in their subjects, who could bear a free, noble brother in their neighborhood without harboring either fear or envy; whose hearts expanded when they saw their table surrounded by their free equals, and who did not think the knights unfit companions till they had degraded themselves by courtly homage.

George.

Have you known such princes?

Goetz.

Ay, truly. As long as I live I shall recollect how the Landgrave of Hanau made a grand hunting-party, and the princes and free feudatories dined under the open heaven, and the country-people all thronged to see them; it was no selfish masquerade instituted for his own private pleasure or vanity. To see the great round-headed peasant lads and the pretty brown girls, the sturdy hinds, and the venerable old men, a crowd of happy faces, all as merry as if they rejoiced in the splendor of their master, which he shared with them under God's free sky!

George.

He must have been as good a master as you.

Goetz.

And may we not hope that many such will rule together some future day, to whom reverence to the emperor, peace and friendship with their neighbors, and the love of their vassals, shall be the best and dearest family treasure handed down to their children's children? Every one will then keep and improve his own, instead of reckoning nothing as gain that is not stolen from his neighbors.

George.

And should we have no more forays?

Goetz.

Would to God there were no restless spirits in all Germany!— we should still have enough to do! We would clear the mountains of wolves, and bring our peaceable laborious neighbor a dish of game from the wood, and eat it together. Were that not full employment, we would join our brethren, and, like cherubims with flaming swords, defend the frontiers of the empire against those wolves the Turks, and those foxes the French, and guard for our beloved emperor both extremities of his extensive empire. That would be a life, George! To risk one's head for the safety of all Germany. *(GEORGEsprings up.)* Whither away?

George.

Alas! I forgot we were besieged—besieged by the very emperor; and before we can expose our lives in his defence, we must risk them for our liberty.

Goetz.

Be of good cheer.

*Enter*LERSE.

Lerse.

Freedom! freedom! The cowardly poltroons—the hesitating, irresolute asses! You are to depart with men, weapons, horses and armor; provisions you are to leave behind.

Goetz.

They will hardly find enough to exercise their jaws.
Lerse.
(*Aside to*GOETZ.) Have you hidden the plate and money?
Goetz.
No! Wife, go with Lerse; he has something to tell thee.
[*Exeunt.*

SCENE XIX. —

The Court of the Castle.
GEORGE.(*In the stable. Sings.*)

An urchin once, as I have heard,
Ha! ha!
Had caught and caged a little bird,
Sa! sa!
Ha! ha!
Sa! sa!

He viewed the prize with heart elate,
Ha! ha!
Thrust in his hand — ah, treacherous fate!
Sa! sa!
Ha! ha!
Sa! sa!

Away the titmouse wing'd its flight,
Ha! ha!
And laugh'd to scorn the silly wight,
Sa! sa!
Ha! ha!
Sa! sa!
*Enter*GOETZ.
Goetz.
How goes it?

George.

(Brings out his horse.) All saddled!

Goetz.

Thou art quick.

George.

As the bird escaped from the cage.

Enter all the besieged.

Goetz.

Have you all your rifles? Not yet! Go, take the best from the armory, 'tis all one; we'll ride on in advance.

George.

(Sings.)

Ha! ha!

Sa! sa!

Ha! ha!

SCENE XX.

The Armory.

Two TROOPERS *choosing guns.*

First Trooper.

I'll have this one.

Second Trooper.

And I this — but yonder's a better.

First Trooper.

Never mind — make haste.

[*Tumult and firing without.*

Second Trooper.

Hark!

First Trooper.

(Springs to the window.) Good heavens, they are murdering our master! He is unhorsed! George is down!

Second Trooper.

How shall we get off? Over the wall by the walnut tree, and into the field.

[*Exit.*

First Trooper.

Lerse keeps his ground; I will to him. If they die, I will not survive them.

[*Exit.*

ACT IV.

SCENE I. —

An Inn in the city of Heilbronn

GOETZ.*(Solus.)*
Goetz.
I am like the evil spirit whom the capuchin conjured into a sack. I fret and labor but all in vain. The perjured villains! (*Enter*ELIZABETH.) What news, Elizabeth, of my dear, my trusty followers?
Elizabeth.
Nothing certain: some are slain, some are prisoners; no one could or would tell me further particulars.
Goetz.
Is this the reward of fidelity, of filial obedience? — "That it may be well with thee, and that thy days may be long in the land!"
Elizabeth.
Dear husband, murmur not against our Heavenly Father. They have their reward. It was born with them — a noble and generous heart. Even in the dungeon they are free. Pay attention to the imperial commissioners; their heavy gold chains become them —
Goetz.
As a necklace becomes a sow! I should like to see George and Lerse in fetters!
Elizabeth.
It were a sight to make angels weep.
Goetz.

I would not weep—I would clench my teeth, and gnaw my lip in fury. What! in fetters! Had ye but loved me less, dear lads! I could never look at them enough—What! to break their word pledged in the name of the emperor!

Elizabeth.

Put away these thoughts. Reflect; you must appear before the council—you are in no mood to meet them, and I fear the worst.

Goetz.

What harm can they do me?

Elizabeth.

Here comes the sergeant.

Goetz.

What! the ass of justice that carries the sacks to the mill and the dung to the field? What now?

Enter SERGEANT.

Sergeant.

The lords commissioners are at the council-house, and require your presence.

Goetz.

I come.

Sergeant.

I am to escort you.

Goetz.

Too much honor.

Elizabeth.

Be but cool.

Goetz.

Fear nothing.

[*Exeunt.*

SCENE II.—

The Council-House at Heilbronn.

*The*IMPERIAL COMMISSIONERS*seated at a table. The*CAPTAIN*and the*MAGISTRATES*of the city attending.*

Magistrate.

In pursuance of your order we have collected the stoutest and most determined of our citizens. They are at hand, in order, at a nod from you, to seize Berlichingen.

Commissioner.

We shall have much pleasure in communicating to his imperial majesty the zeal with which you have obeyed his illustrious commands. — Are they artisans?

Magistrate.

Smiths, coopers and carpenters, men with hands hardened by labor; and resolute here.

[*Points to his breast.*

Commissioner.

'Tis well.

*Enter*SERGEANT.

Sergeant.

Goetz von Berlichingen waits without.

Commissioner.

Admit him.

*Enter*GOETZ.

Goetz.

God save you, sirs! What would you with me?

Commissioner.

First, that you consider where you are; and in whose presence.

Goetz.

By my faith, I know you right well, sirs.

Commissioner.

You acknowledge allegiance.

Goetz.

With all my heart.

Commissioner.

Be seated.

[*Points to a stool.*

Goetz.

What, down there? I'd rather stand. That stool smells so of poor sinners, as indeed does the whole apartment.

Commissioner.

Stand, then.

Goetz.

To business, if you please.

Commissioner.

We shall proceed in due order.

Goetz.

I am glad to hear it. Would you had always done so.

Commissioner.

You know how you fell into our hands, and are a prisoner at discretion.

Goetz.

What will you give me to forget it?

Commissioner.

Could I give you modesty, I should better your affairs.

Goetz.

Better my affairs! could you but do that? To repair is more difficult than to destroy.

Secretary.

Shall I put all this on record?

Commissioner.

Only what is to the purpose.

Goetz.

As far as I'm concerned you may print every word of it.

Commissioner.

You fell into the power of the emperor whose paternal goodness got the better of his justice, and, instead of throwing you into a dungeon, ordered you to repair to his beloved city of Heilbronn. You gave your knightly parole to appear, and await the termination in all humility.

Goetz.

Well; I am here, and await it.

Commissioner.

And we are here to intimate to you his imperial majesty's mercy and clemency. He is pleased to forgive your rebellion, to release you from the ban and all well-merited punishment; provided you do, with becoming humility, receive his bounty, and subscribe to the articles which shall be read unto you.

Goetz.

I am his majesty's faithful servant, as ever. One word ere you proceed. My people—where are they? What will be done with them?

ARTIST: A. WAGNER.
GÖTZ VON BERLICHINGEN. ACT IV.
THE ATTEMPTED ARREST OF GÖTZ.

Commissioner.

That concerns you not.

Goetz.

So may the emperor turn his face from you in the hour of your need. They were my comrades, and are so now. What have you done with them?

Commissioner.

We are not bound to account to you.

Goetz.

Ah! I forgot that you are not even pledged to perform what you have promised, much less—

Commissioner.

Our business is to lay the articles before you. Submit yourself to the emperor, and you may find a way to petition for the life and freedom of your comrades.

Goetz.

Your paper.

Commissioner.

Secretary, read it.

Secretary.

(*Reads.*) "I, Goetz of Berlichingen, make public acknowledgment, by these presents, that I, having lately risen in rebellion against the emperor and empire—"

Goetz.

'Tis false! I am no rebel, I have committed no offence against the emperor, and with the empire I have no concern.

Commissioner.

Be silent, and hear further.

Goetz.

I will hear no further. Let any one arise and bear witness. Have I ever taken one step against the emperor, or against the House of Austria? Has not the whole tenor of my conduct proved that I feel better than any one else what all Germany owes to its head; and especially what the free knights and feudatories owe to their liege lord the emperor? I should be a villain could I be induced to subscribe that paper.

Commissioner.

Yet we have strict orders to try and persuade you by fair means, or, in case of your refusal, to throw you into prison.

Goetz.

Into prison! — Me?

Commissioner.

Where you may expect your fate from the hands of justice, since you will not take it from those of mercy.

Goetz.

To prison! You abuse the imperial power! To prison! That was not the emperor's command. What, ye traitors, to dig a pit for me, and hang out your oath, your knightly honor as the bait? To promise me permission to ward myself on parole, and then again to break your treaty!

Commissioner.

We owe no faith to robbers.

Goetz.

Wert thou not the representative of my sovereign, whom I respect even in the vilest counterfeit, thou should'st swallow that word, or choke upon it. I was engaged in an honorable feud. Thou mightest thank God, and magnify thyself before the world, hadst thou ever done as gallant a deed as that with which I now stand charged.*(The*COMMISSIONER*makes a sign* *to the*MAGISTRATE*of Heilbronn, who rings a bell.*) Not for the sake of paltry gain, not to wrest followers or lands from the weak and the defenceless, have I sallied forth. To rescue my page and defend my own person—see ye any rebellion in that? The emperor and his magnates, reposing on their pillows, would never have felt our need. I have, God be praised, one hand left, and I have done well to use it.

*Enter a party of*ARTISANS*armed with halberds and swords.*

Goetz.

What means this?

Commissioner.

You will not listen.—Seize him!

Goetz.

Let none come near me who is not a very Hungarian ox. One salutation from my iron fist shall cure him of headache, toothache and every other ache under the wide heaven! *(They rush upon him. He strikes one down; and snatches a sword from another. They stand aloof.)* Come on! come on! I should like to become acquainted with the bravest among you.

Commissioner.

Surrender!

Goetz.

With a sword in my hand! Know ye not that it depends but upon myself to make way through all these hares and gain the open field? But I will teach you how a man should keep his word. Promise me but free ward, and I will give up my sword, and am again your prisoner.

Commissioner.

How! Would you treat with the emperor, sword in hand?

Goetz.

God forbid!—only with you and your worthy fraternity! You may go home, good people; you are only losing your time, and here there is nothing to be got but bruises.

Commissioner.

Seize him! What! does not your love for the emperor supply you with courage?

Goetz.

No more than the emperor supplies them with plaster for the wounds their courage would earn them.

Enter SERGEANT *hastily.*

Officer.

The warder has just discovered from the castle-tower a troop of more than two hundred horsemen hastening towards the town. Unperceived by us, they have pressed forward from behind the hill, and threaten our walls

Commissioner.

Alas! alas! What can this mean?

A SOLDIER *enters.*

Soldier.

Francis of Sickingen waits at the drawbridge, and informs you that he has heard how perfidiously you have broken your word to his brother-in-law, and how the Council of Heilbronn have aided and abetted in the treason. He is now come to insist upon justice, and if refused it, threatens, within an hour, to fire the four quarters of your town, and abandon it to be plundered by his vassals.

Goetz.

My gallant brother!

Commissioner.

Withdraw, Goetz. (*Exit* GOETZ.) What is to be done?

Magistrate.

Have compassion upon us and our town! Sickingen is inexorable in his wrath; he will keep his word.

Commissioner.

Shall we forget what is due to ourselves and the emperor?

Captain.

If we had but men to enforce it; but situated as we are, a show of resistance would only make matters worse. It is better for us to yield.

Magistrate.

Let us apply to Goetz to put in a good word for us. I feel as though I saw the town already in flames.

Commissioner.

Let Goetz approach.

*Enter*GOETZ.

Goetz.

What now?

Commissioner.

Thou wilt do well to dissuade thy brother-in-law from his rebellious interference. Instead of rescuing thee, he will only plunge thee deeper in destruction, and become the companion of thy fall!

Goetz.

(Sees Elizabeth at the door, and speaks to her aside.) Go; tell him instantly to break in and force his way hither, but to spare the town. As for these rascals, if they offer any resistance, let him use force. I care not if I lose my life, provided they are all knocked on the head at the same time.

SCENE III. —

*A large Hall in the Council-House, beset by*SICKINGEN'S*Troops. Enter*SICKINGEN*and*GOETZ.

Goetz.

That was help from heaven. How camest thou so opportunely and unexpectedly, brother?

Sickingen.

Without witchcraft. I had despatched two or three messengers to learn how it fared with thee; when I beard of the perjury of these fellows I set out instantly, and now we have them safe.

Goetz.

I ask nothing but knightly ward upon my parole.

Sickingen.

You are too noble. Not even to avail yourself of the advantage which the honest man has over the perjurer! They are in the wrong, and we will not give them cushions to sit upon. They have shamefully abused the imperial authority, and, if I know anything of the emperor, you might safely insist upon more favorable terms. You ask too little.

Goetz.

I have ever been content with little.

Sickingen.

And therefore that little has always been denied thee. My proposal is, that they shall release your servants, and permit you all to return to your castle on parole—you can promise not to leave it till the emperor's pleasure be known. You will be safer there than here.

Goetz.

They will say my property is escheated to the emperor.

Sickingen.

Then we will answer thou canst dwell there, and keep it for his service till he restores it to thee again. Let them wriggle like eels in the net, they shall not escape us! They may talk of the imperial dignity—of their commission. We will not mind that. I know the emperor, and have some influence with him. He has ever wished to have thee in his service. You will not be long in your castle without being summoned to serve him.

Goetz.

God grant it, ere I forget the use of arms!

Sickingen.

Valor can never be forgotten, as it can never be learned. Fear nothing! When thy affairs are settled, I will repair to court, where my enterprises begin to ripen. Good fortune seems to smile on them. I want only to sound the emperor's mind. The towns of Triers and Pfalz as soon expect that the sky should fall, as that I shall come down upon their heads. But I will come like a hailstorm! and if I am successful, thou shalt soon be brother to an elector. I had hoped for thy assistance in this undertaking.

Goetz.

(Looks at his hand.) Oh! that explains the dream I had the night before I promised Maria to Weislingen. I thought he vowed eternal fidelity, and held my iron hand so fast that it loosened from the arm. Alas! I am at this moment more defenceless than when it was shot away. Weislingen! Weislingen!

Sickingen.

Forget the traitor! We will thwart his plans, and undermine his authority, till shame and remorse shall gnaw him to death. I see, I see the downfall of our enemies. — Goetz — only half a year more!

Goetz.

Thy soul soars high! I know not why, but for some time past no fair prospects have dawned upon me. I have been ere now it sore distress — I have been a prisoner before — but never did I experience such a depression.

Sickingen.

Fortune gives courage. Come, let us to the bigwigs. They have had time enough to deliberate, let us take the trouble upon ourselves.

[*Exeunt.*

SCENE IV. —

The Castle of ADELAIDE. *Augsburg.*
ADELAIDE *and* WEISLINGEN *discovered.*

Adelaide.

This is detestable.

Weislingen.

I have gnashed my teeth. So good a plan — so well followed out — and after all to leave him in possession of his castle! That cursed Sickingen!

Adelaide.

The council should not have consented.

Weislingen.

They were in the net. What else could they do? Sickingen threatened them with fire and sword, —the haughty, vindictive man! I hate him! His power waxes like a mountain torrent—let it but gain a few brooks, and others come pouring to its aid.

Adelaide.

Have they no emperor?

Weislingen.

My dear wife, he waxes old and feeble; he is only the shadow of what he was. When he heard what had been done, and I and the other counsellors murmured indignantly: "Let them alone!" said he; "I can spare my old Goetz his little fortress, and if he remains quiet there, what have you to say against him?" We spoke of the welfare of the state. "Oh," said he, "that I had always had counsellors who would have urged my restless spirit to consult more the happiness of individuals?"

Adelaide.

He has lost the spirit of a prince!

Weislingen.

We inveighed against Sickingen!—"He is my faithful servant," said he; "and if he has not acted by my express order, he has performed what I wished better than my plenipotentiaries, and I can ratify what he has done as well after as before."

Adelaide.

'Tis enough to drive one mad.

Weislingen.

Yet I have not given up all hope. Goetz is on parole to remain quiet in his castle. 'Tis impossible for him to keep his promise, and we shall soon have some new cause of complaint.

Adelaide.

That is the more likely, as we may hope that the old emperor will soon leave the world, and Charles, his gallant successor, will display a more princely mind.

Weislingen.

Charles! He is neither chosen nor crowned.

Adelaide.

Who does not expect and hope for that event?

Weislingen.

You have a great idea of his abilities; one might almost think you looked on him with partial eyes.

Adelaide.

You insult me, Weislingen. For what do you take me?

Weislingen.

I do not mean to offend; but I cannot be silent upon the subject. Charles' marked attentions to you disquiet me.

Adelaide.

And do I receive them as —

Weislingen.

You are a woman; and no woman hates those who pay their court to her.

Adelaide.

This from you?

Weislingen.

It cuts me to the heart — the dreadful thought — Adelaide.

Adelaide.

Can I not cure thee of this folly?

Weislingen.

If thou would'st; thou canst leave the court.

Adelaide.

But upon what pretence? Art thou not here? Must I leave you and all my friends, to shut myself up with the owls in your solitary castle? No, Weislingen, that will never do; be at rest, thou knowest I love thee.

Weislingen.

That is my anchor so long as the cable holds.

[*Exit.*

Adelaide.

Ah! It is come to this? This was yet wanting. The projects of my bosom are too great to brook the interruption. Charles — the great, the gallant Charles — the future emperor — shall he be the only man unrewarded by my favor? Think not,

Weislingen, to hinder me—else shalt thou to earth; my way lies over thee!

Enter FRANCIS *with a letter.*

Francis.

Here, gracious lady.

Adelaide.

Hadst thou it from Charles' own hand?

Francis.

Yes.

Adelaide.

What ails thee? Thou look'st so mournful!

Francis.

It is your pleasure that I should pine away, and waste my fairest years in agonizing despair.

Adelaide.

(Aside.) I pity him; and how little would it cost me to make him happy. *(Aloud.)* Be of good courage, youth! I know thy love and fidelity, and will not be ungrateful.

Francis.

(With stifled breath.) If thou wert capable of ingratitude, I could not survive it. There boils not a drop of blood in my veins but what is thine own—I have not a single feeling but to love and to serve thee!

Adelaide.

Dear Francis!

Francis.

You flatter me. *(Bursts into tears.)* Does my attachment deserve only to be a stepping stool to another—to see all your thoughts fixed upon Charles?

Adelaide.

You know not what you wish, and still less what you say.

Francis.

(Stamping with vexation and rage.) No more will I be your slave, your go-between!

Adelaide.

Francis, you forget yourself.

Francis.

To sacrifice my beloved master and myself —

Adelaide.

Out of my sight!

Francis.

Gracious lady!

Adelaide.

Go, betray to thy beloved master the secret of my soul! Fool that I was to take thee for what thou art not.

Francis.

Dear lady! you know how I love you.

Adelaide.

And thou, who wast my friend — so near my heart — go, betray me.

Francis.

Rather would I tear my heart from my breast! Forgive me, gentle lady! my heart is too full, my senses desert me.

Adelaide.

Thou dear, affectionate boy! (*She takes him by both hands, draws him towards her and kisses him. He throws himself weeping upon her neck.*) Leave me!

Francis.

(*His voice choked by tears.*) Heavens!

Adelaide.

Leave me! The walls are traitors. Leave me! (*Breaks from him.*) Be but steady in fidelity and love, and the fairest reward is thine.

[*Exit.*

Francis.

The fairest reward! let me but live till that moment — I could murder my father, were he an obstacle to my happiness!

[*Exit.*

SCENE V. —

Jaxthausen.

GOETZ*seated at a table with writing materials.*ELIZABETH*beside him with her work.*

Goetz.

This idle life does not suit me. My confinement becomes more irksome every day; I would I could sleep, or persuade myself that quiet is agreeable.

Elizabeth.

Continue writing the account of thy deeds which thou hast commenced. Give into the hands of thy friends evidence to put thine enemies to shame; make a noble posterity acquainted with thy real character.

Goetz.

Alas! writing is but busy idleness; it wearies me. While I am writing what I have done, I lament the misspent time in which I might do more.

Elizabeth.

(*Takes the writing.*) Be not impatient. Thou hast come to thy first imprisonment at Heilbronn.

Goetz.

That was always an unlucky place to me.

Elizabeth.

(*Reads.*) "There were even some of the confederates who told me that I had acted foolishly in appearing before my bitterest enemies, who, as I might suspect, would not deal justly with me." And what didst thou answer? Write on.

Goetz.

I said, "Have I not often risked life and limb for the welfare and property of others, and shall I not do so for the honor of my knightly word?"

Elizabeth.

Thus does fame speak of thee.

Goetz.

They shall not rob me of my honor. They have taken all else from me — property — liberty — everything.

Elizabeth.

I happened once to stand in an inn near the Lords of Miltenberg and Singlingen, who knew me not. Then I was joyful as at the birth of my first-born; for they extolled thee to each other, and said, — He is the mirror of knighthood, noble and merciful in prosperity, dauntless and true in misfortune.

Goetz.

Let them show me the man to whom I have broken my word. Heaven knows, my ambition has ever been to labor for my neighbor more than for myself, and to acquire the fame of a gallant and irreproachable knight, rather than principalities or power; and, God be praised! I have gained the meed of my labor.

Enter GEORGE *and* LERSE *with game.*

Goetz.

Good luck to my gallant huntsmen!

George.

Such have we become from gallant troopers. Boots can easily be cut down into buskins.

Lerse.

The chase is always something — 'tis a kind of war.

George.

Yes; if we were not always crossed by these imperial gamekeepers. Don't you recollect, my lord, how you prophesied we should become huntsmen when the world was turned topsy-turvy? We are become so now without waiting for that.

Goetz.

'Tis all the same, we are pushed out of our sphere.

George.

These are wonderful times! For eight days a dreadful comet has been seen — all Germany fears that it portends the death of the emperor, who is very ill.

Goetz.

Very ill! Then our career draws to a close.

Lerse.

And in the neighborhood there are terrible commotions; the peasants have made a formidable insurrection.

Goetz.

Where?

Lerse.

In the heart of Swabia; they are plundering, burning and slaying. I fear they will sack the whole country.

George.

It is a horrible warfare! They have already risen in a hundred places, and daily increase in number. A hurricane too has lately torn up the whole forests; and in the place where the insurrection began, two fiery swords have been seen in the sky crossing each other.

Goetz.

Then some of my poor friends and neighbors no doubt suffer innocently.

George.

Alas! that we are pent up thus!

ACT V.

SCENE I. —

A Village plundered by the insurgent Peasantry. Shrieks and tumult.
WOMEN, OLD MEN*and*CHILDREN*fly across the Stage.*
Old Man.
Away! away! let us fly from the murdering dogs.
Woman.
Sacred heaven! How blood-red is the sky! how blood-red the setting sun!
Another.
That must be fire.
A Third.
My husband! my husband!
Old Man.
Away! away! To the wood!
[*Exeunt.*
*Enter*LINK*and*INSURGENTS.
Link.
Whoever opposes you, down with him! The village is ours. Let none of the booty be injured, none be left behind. Plunder clean and quickly. We must soon set fire—
*Enter*METZLER,*coming down the hill.*
Metzler.
How do things go with you, Link?

ARTIST: A. WAGNER.
GÖTZ VON BERLICHINGEN. ACT V.

Link.

Merrily enough, as you see; you are just in time for the fun. — Whence come you?

Metzler.

From Weinsberg. There was a jubilee.

Link.

How so?

Metzler.

We stabbed them all, in such heaps it was a joy to see it!

Link.

All whom?

Metzler.

Dietrich von Weiler led up the dance. The fool! We were all raging around the church steeple. He looked out and wished to treat with us. — Baf! A ball through his head! Up we rushed like a tempest, and the fellow soon made his exit by the window.

Link.

Huzza!

Metzler.

(To thePEASANTS.) Ye dogs, must I find you legs? How they gape and loiter, the asses!

Link.

Set fire! Let them roast in the flames! forward! Push on, ye dolts.

Metzler.

Then we brought out Helfenstein, Eltershofen, thirteen of the nobility — eighty in all. They were led out on the plain before Heilbronn. What a shouting and jubilee among our lads as the long row of miserable sinners passed by! they stared at each other, and, heaven and earth! we surrounded them before they were aware, and then despatched them all with our pikes.

Link.

Why was I not there?

Metzler.

Never in all my life did I see such fun.

Link.

On! on! Bring all out!

Peasant.

All's clear.

Link.

Then fire the village at the four corners.

Metzler.

'Twill make a fine bonfire! Hadst thou but seen how the fellows tumbled over one another, and croaked like frogs! It warmed my heart like a cup of brandy. One Rexinger was there, a fellow, with a white plume and flaxen locks, who, when he went out hunting, used to drive us before him like dogs, and with dogs. I had not caught sight of him all the while, when suddenly his fool's visage looked me full in the face. Push! went the spear between his ribs, and there he lay stretched on all-fours above his companions. The fellows lay kicking in a heap like the hares that used to be driven together at their grand hunting parties.

Link.

It smokes finely already!

Metzler.

Yonder it burns! Come, let us with the booty to the main body.

Link.

Where do they halt?

Metzler.

Between this and Heilbronn. They wish to choose a captain whom every one will respect, for we are after all only their equals; they feel this, and turn restive.

Link.

Whom do they propose?

Metzler.

Maximilian Stumf, or Goetz von Berlichingen.

Link.

That would be well. 'Twould give the thing credit should Goetz accept it. He has ever been held a worthy independent knight. Away, away! We march towards Heilbronn! Pass the word.

Metzler.

The fire will light us a good part of the way. Hast thou seen the great comet?

Link.

Yes. It is a dreadful ghastly sign! As we march by night we can see it well. It rises about one o'clock.

Metzler.

And is visible but for an hour and a quarter, like an arm brandishing a sword, and bloody red!

Link.

Didst thou mark the three stars at the sword's hilt and point?

Metzler.

And the broad haze-colored stripe illuminated by a thousand streamers like lances, and between them little swords.

Link.

I shuddered with horror. The sky was pale red streaked with ruddy flames, and among them grisly figures with shaggy hair and beards.

Metzler.

Did you see them too? And how they all swam about as though in a sea of blood, and struggled in confusion, enough to turn one's brain.

Link.

Away! away!

[*Exeunt.*

SCENE II. —

Open Country. In the distance two Villages and an Abbey are burning.

KOHL, WILD, MAXIMILIAN. STUMF.*Insurgents.*

Stumf.

You cannot ask me to be your leader; it were bad for you and for me: I am a vassal of the palsgrave, and how shall I make war against my liege lord? Besides, you would always suspect I did not act from my heart.

Kohl.

We knew well thou would'st make some excuse.

*Enter*GEORGE, LERSE*and*GOETZ.

Goetz.

What would you with me?

Kohl.

You must be our captain.

Goetz.

How can I break my knightly word to the emperor. I am under the ban: I cannot quit my territory.

Wild.

That's no excuse.

Goetz.

And were I free, and you wanted to deal with the lords and nobles as you did at Weinsberg, laying waste the country round with fire and sword, and should wish me to be an abettor of your shameless, barbarous doings, rather than be your captain, you should slay me like a mad dog!

Kohl.

What has been done cannot be undone.

Stumf.

That was just the misfortune, that they had no leader whom they honored, and who could bridle their fury. I beseech thee, Goetz, accept the office! The princes will be grateful; all Germany will thank thee. It will be for the weal and prosperity of all. The country and its inhabitants will be preserved.

Goetz.

Why dost not thou accept it?

Stumf.

I have given them reasons for my refusal.

Kohl.

We have no time to waste in useless speeches. Once for all! Goetz, be our chief, or look to thy castle and thy head! Take two hours to consider of it. Guard him!

Goetz.

To what purpose? I am as resolved now as I shall ever be. Why have ye risen up in arms? If to recover your rights and freedom, why do you plunder and lay waste the land? Will you abstain from such evil doings, and act as true men who know what they want? Then will I be your chief for eight days, and help you in your lawful and orderly demands.

Wild.

What has been done was done in the first heat, and thy interference is not needed to prevent it for the future.

Kohl.

Thou must engage with us at least for a quarter of a year.

Stumf.

Say four weeks, that will satisfy both parties.

Goetz.

Then be it so.

Kohl.

Your hand!

Goetz.

But you must promise to send the treaty you have made with me in writing to all your troops, and to punish severely those who infringe it.

Wild.

Well, it shall be done.

Goetz.

Then I bind myself to you for four weeks.

Stumf.

Good fortune to you! In whatever thou doest, spare our noble lord the palsgrave.

Kohl.

(*Aside.*) See that none speak to him without our knowledge.

Goetz.

Lerse, go to my wife. Protect her; you shall soon have news of me.

[*Exeunt*GOETZ, STUMF, GEORGE, LERSE*and some*PEASANTS.

*Enter*METZLER, LINK*and their followers.*

Metzler.

Who talks of a treaty? What's the use of a treaty?

Link.

It is shameful to make any such bargain.

Kohl.

We know as well what we want as you; and we may do or let alone what we please.

Wild.

This raging, and burning, and murdering must have an end some day or other; and by renouncing it just now, we gain a brave leader.

Metzler.

How? An end? Thou traitor! why are we here but to avenge ourselves on our enemies, and enrich ourselves at their expense? Some prince's slave has been tampering with thee.

Kohl.

Come, Wild, he is like a brute-beast.

[*Exeunt*WILD*and*KOHL.

Metzler.

Ay, go your way; no band will stick by you. The villains! Link, we'll set on the others to burn Miltenberg yonder; and if they begin a quarrel about the treaty, we'll cut off the heads of those that made it.

Link.

We have still the greater body of peasants on our side.

[*Exeunt with*INSURGENTS.

SCENE III. —

A Hill and Prospect of the Country. In the flat scene a Mill. A body of Horsemen.
WEISLINGEN*comes out of the Mill, followed by*FRANCIS*and a*COURIER.
Weislingen.
My horse! Have you announced it to the other nobles?
Courier.
At least seven standards will meet you in the wood behind Miltenberg. The peasants are marching in that direction. Couriers are despatched on all sides; the entire confederacy will soon be assembled. Our plan cannot fail; and they say there is dissension among them.
Weislingen.
So much the better. Francis!
Francis.
Gracious sir!
Weislingen.
Discharge thine errand punctually. I bind it upon thy soul. Give her the letter. She shall from the court to my castle instantly. Thou must see her depart, and bring me notice of it.
Francis.
Your commands shall be obeyed.
Weislingen.
Tell her she *shall* go. (*To the*COURIER.) Lead us by the nearest and best road.
Courier.
We must go round; all the rivers are swollen with the late heavy rains.

SCENE IV. —

Jaxthausen.
ELIZABETH*and*LERSE.

Lerse.

Gracious lady, be comforted!

Elizabeth.

Alas! Lerse, the tears stood in his eyes when he took leave of me. It is dreadful, dreadful!

Lerse.

He will return.

Elizabeth.

It is not that. When he went forth to gain honorable victories, never did grief sit heavy at my heart. I then rejoiced in the prospect of his return, which I now dread.

Lerse.

So noble a man.

Elizabeth.

Call him not so. There lies the new misery. The miscreants! they threatened to murder his family and burn his castle. Should he return, gloomy, most gloomy shall I see his brow. His enemies will forge scandalous accusations against him, which he will be unable to refute.

Lerse.

He will and can.

Elizabeth.

He has broken his parole — canst thou deny that?

Lerse.

No! he was constrained; what reason is there to condemn him?

Elizabeth.

Malice seeks not reasons, but pretexts. He has become an ally of rebels, malefactors and murderers: he has become their chief. Say No to that.

Lerse.

Cease to torment yourself and me. Have they not solemnly sworn to abjure all such doings as those at Weinsberg? Did I not myself hear them say, in remorse, that, had not that been done already, it never should have been done? Must not the princes and nobles return him their best thanks for having undertaken the dangerous office of leading these unruly people, in order to restrain their rage, and to save so many lives and possessions?

Elizabeth.

Thou art an affectionate advocate. Should they take him prisoner, deal with him as with a rebel, and bring his gray hairs— Lerse, I should go mad!

Lerse.

Send sleep to refresh her body, dear Father of mankind, if Thou deniest comfort to her soul!

Elizabeth.

George has promised to bring news, but he will not be allowed to do so. They are worse than prisoners. Well I know they are watched like enemies.—The gallant boy! he would not leave his master.

Lerse.

The very heart within me bled as I left him.—Had you not needed my help, all the terrors of grisly death should not have separated us.

Elizabeth.

I know not where Sickingen is.—Could I but send a message to Maria!

Lerse.

Write, then. I will take care that she receives it.

[*Exit.*

SCENE V. —

A Village.

Enter GOETZ *and* GEORGE.

Goetz.

To horse, George! Quick! I see Miltenberg in flames. Is it thus they keep the treaty?—Ride to them, tell them my purpose.—The murderous incendiaries—I renounce them.— Let them make a thieving gypsy their captain, not me!—

Quick, George! (*Exit* GEORGE.) Would that I were a thousand miles hence, at the bottom of the deepest dungeon in Turkey!—Could I but come off with honor from them! I have thwarted them every day, and told them the bitterest truths, in the hope they might weary of me and let me go.

Enter an UNKNOWN.

Unknown.

God save you, gallant sir!

Goetz.

I thank you! What is your errand? Your name?

Unknown.

My name does not concern my business. I come to tell you that your life is in danger. The insurgent leaders are weary of hearing from you such harsh language, and are resolved to rid themselves of you. Speak them fair, or endeavor to escape from them; and God be with you!

[*Exit.*

Goetz.

To quit life in this fashion, Goetz, to end thus? But be it so. My death will be the clearest proof to the world that I have had nothing in common with the miscreants.

Enter INSURGENTS.

First Insurgent.

Captain, they are prisoners, they are slain!

Goetz.

Who?

Second Insurgent.

Those who burned Miltenberg; a troop of confederate cavalry suddenly charged upon them from behind the hill.

Goetz.

They have their reward. O George! George! They have taken him prisoner with the caitiffs.—My George! my George!

Enter INSURGENTS *in confusion.*

Link.

Up, sir captain, up!—There is no time to lose—the enemy is at hand, and in force.

Goetz.

Who burned Miltenberg?

Metzler.

If you mean to pick a quarrel, we'll soon show you how we'll end it.

Kohl.

Look to your own safety and ours. — Up!

Goetz.

(*To*METZLER.) Darest thou threaten me, thou scoundrel? — Thinkest thou to awe me, because thy garments are stained with the Count of Helfenstein's blood?

Metzler.

Berlichingen!

Goetz.

Thou mayest call me by my name, and my children will not be ashamed to hear it.

Metzler.

Out upon thee, coward! — Prince's slave!

[GOETZ*strikes him down. — The others interpose.*

Kohl.

Ye are mad! — The enemy are breaking in on all sides, and you quarrel!

Link.

Away! away! [*Cries and tumult. — The*INSURGENTS*fly across the stage.*

*Enter*WEISLINGEN*and*TROOPERS.

Weislingen.

Pursue! pursue! they fly! — Stop neither for darkness nor rain. — I hear Goetz is among them; look that he escape you not. Our friends say he is sorely wounded.(*Exeunt*TROOPERS.) And when I have caught thee — it will be merciful secretly to execute the sentence of death in prison. Thus he perishes from the memory of man, and then, foolish heart, thou mayest beat more freely.

SCENE VI. —

The front of a Gypsy-hut in a wild forest. — Night. — A fire before the hut, at which are seated the MOTHER OF THE GYPSIES *and a girl.*

Mother.

Throw some fresh straw upon the thatch, daughter: there'll be heavy rain again to-night.

Enter a GYPSY-BOY.

Boy.

A dormouse, mother! and look! two field-mice!

Mother.

I'll skin them and roast them for thee, and thou shalt have a cap of their skins. Thou bleedest!

Boy.

Dormouse bit me.

Mother.

Fetch some dead wood, that the fire may burn bright when thy father comes: he will be wet through and through.

Another GYPSY-WOMAN *with a child at her back.*

First Woman.

Hast thou had good luck?

Second Woman.

Ill enough. The whole country is in an uproar; one's life is not safe a moment. Two villages are in a blaze.

First Woman.

Is it fire that glares so yonder? I have been watching it long. One is so accustomed now to fiery signs in the heavens.

The CAPTAIN OF THE GYPSIES *enters with three of his gang.*

Captain.

Heard ye the wild huntsman?

First Woman.

He is passing over us now.

Captain.

How the hounds give tongue! Wow! wow!

Second Man.

How the whips crack!

Third Man.

And the huntsmen cheer them. — Hallo — ho!

Mother.

'Tis the devil's chase.

Captain.

We have been fishing in troubled waters. The peasants rob each other; there's no harm in our helping them.

Second Woman.

What hast thou got, Wolf?

Wolf.

A hare and a capon, a spit, a bundle of linen, three spoons and a bridle.

Sticks.

I have a blanket and a pair of boots, also a flint and tinder-box.

Mother.

All wet as mire; I'll dry them, give them here!

[*Tramping without.*

Captain.

Hark! — A horse! Go see who it is.

Enter GOETZ *on horseback.*

Goetz.

I thank thee, God! I see fire — they are gypsies. — My wounds bleed sorely — my foes are close behind me! — Great God, this is a fearful end!

Captain.

Is it in peace thou comest?

Goetz.

I crave help from you — my wounds exhaust me — assist me to dismount!

Captain.

Help him! — A gallant warrior in look and speech.

Wolf.

(*Aside.*) 'Tis Goetz von Berlichingen!

Captain.

Welcome! welcome! — All that we have is yours.

Goetz.

Thanks, thanks!

Captain.

Come to my hut!

[*Exeunt to the hut.*

SCENE VII. —

Inside the Hut.

CAPTAIN, GYPSIES*and*GOETZ.

Captain.

Call our mother — tell her to bring bloodwort and bandages. (GOETZ*unarms himself.*) Here is my holiday doublet.

Goetz.

God reward you!

[*The*MOTHER*binds his wounds.*

Captain.

I rejoice that you are come.

Goetz.

Do you know me?

Captain.

Who does not know you, Goetz? Our lives and heart's blood are yours.

*Enter*STICKS.

Sticks.

Horsemen are coming through the wood. They are confederates.

Captain.

Your pursuers! They shall not harm you. Away, Sticks, call the others: we know the passes better than they. We shall shoot them ere they are aware of us.

[*Exeunt*CAPTAIN*and*MEN-GYPSIES*with their guns.*

Goetz.

(Alone.) O Emperor! Emperor! Robbers protect thy children. *(A sharp firing.)* The wild foresters! Steady and true!

Enter WOMEN.

Women.

Flee! flee! The enemy has overpowered us.

Goetz.

Where is my horse?

Women.

Here!

Goetz.

(Girds on his sword and mounts without his armor.) For the last time shall you feel my arm. I am not so weak yet.

[*Exit. – Tumult.*

Women.

He gallops to join our party.

[*Firing.*

Enter WOLF.

Wolf.

Away! Away! All is lost. — The captain is shot! — Goetz a prisoner.

[*The* WOMEN *scream and fly into the wood.*

SCENE VIII. —

ADELAIDE'S *Bedchamber.*

Enter ADELAIDE *with a letter.*

Adelaide.

He or I! The tyrant — to threaten me! We will anticipate him. Who glides through the ante-chamber? *(A low knock at the door.)* Who is there?

Francis.

(In a low voice.) Open, gracious lady!

Adelaide.

Francis! He well deserves that I should admit him.

[*Opens the door.*

Francis.

(Throws himself on her neck.) My dear, my gracious lady!

Adelaide.

What audacity! If any one should hear you?

Francis.

Oh—all—all are asleep.

Adelaide.

What would'st thou?

Francis.

I cannot rest. The threats of my master.—your fate,—my heart.

Adelaide.

He was incensed against me when you parted from him?

Francis.

He was as I have never seen him.—To my castle, said he, she must—she *shall* go.

Adelaide.

And shall we obey?

Francis.

I know not, dear lady!

Adelaide.

Thou foolish, infatuated boy! Thou dost not see where this will end. Here he knows I am in safety. He has long had designs on my freedom, and therefore wishes to get me to his castle—there he will have power to use me as his hate shall dictate.

Francis.

He shall not!

Adelaide.

Wilt thou prevent him?

Francis.

He shall not!

Adelaide.

I foresee the whole misery of my fate. He will tear me forcibly from his castle to immure me in a cloister.

Francis.

Hell and damnation!

Adelaide.

Wilt thou rescue me?

Francis.

Anything! Everything!

Adelaide.

(Throws herself weeping upon his neck.) Francis! O save me!

Francis.

He shall fall. I will plant my foot upon his neck.

Adelaide.

No violence! You shall carry a submissive letter to him announcing obedience — then give him this vial in his wine.

Francis.

Give it me! Thou shalt be free!

Adelaide.

Free! — And then no more shalt thou need to come to my chamber trembling and in fear. No more shall I need anxiously to say, "Away, Francis! the morning dawns."

SCENE IX. —

Street before the Prison at Heilbronn.

ELIZABETHandLERSE.

Lerse.

Heaven relieve your distress, gracious lady! Maria is come.

Elizabeth.

God be praised! Lerse, we have sunk into dreadful misery. My worst forebodings are realized! A prisoner — thrown as an assassin and malefactor into the deepest dungeon.

Lerse.

I know all.

Elizabeth.

Thou knowest nothing. Our distress is too — too great! His age, his wounds, a slow fever — and, more than all, the despondency of his mind to think that this should be his end.

Lerse.

Ay, and that Weislingen should be commissioner!
Elizabeth.
Weislingen?
Lerse.
They have acted with unheard-of severity. Metzler has been burned alive—hundreds of his associates broken upon the wheel, beheaded, quartered and impaled. All the country round looks like a slaughter-house, where human flesh is cheap.
Elizabeth.
Weislingen commissioner! O Heaven! a ray of hope! Maria shall go to him: he cannot refuse her. He had ever a compassionate heart, and when he sees her whom he once loved so much, whom he has made so miserable—where is she?
Lerse.
Still at the inn.
Elizabeth.
Take me to her. She must away instantly. I fear the worst.
[*Exeunt.*

SCENE X. —

*An Apartment in*WEISLINGEN'S*Castle.*

Weislingen.
(*Alone.*) I am so ill, so weak—all my bones are hollow—this wretched fever has consumed their very marrow. No rest, no sleep, by day or night! and when I slumber, such fearful dreams! Last night methought I met Goetz in the forest. He drew his sword, and defied me to combat. I grasped mine, but my hand failed me. He darted on me a look of contempt, sheathed his weapon, and passed on. He is a prisoner; yet I tremble to think of him. Miserable man! Thine own voice has condemned him; yet thou tremblest like a malefactor at his

very shadow. And shall he die? Goetz! Goetz! we mortals are not our own masters. Fiends have empire over us, and shape our actions after their own hellish will, to goad us to perdition. *(Sits down.)* Weak! Weak! Why are my nails so blue? A cold, clammy, wasting sweat drenches every limb. Everything swims before my eyes. Could I but sleep! Alas! *Enter*MARIA.

Weislingen.

Mother of God! Leave me in peace—leave me in peace! This spectre was yet wanting. Maria is dead, and she appears to the traitor. Leave me, blessed spirit! I am wretched enough.

Maria.

Weislingen, I am no spirit. I am Maria.

Weislingen.

It is her voice!

Maria.

I came to beg my brother's life of thee. He is guiltless, however culpable he may appear.

Weislingen.

Hush! Maria—angel of heaven as thou art, thou bringest with thee the torments of hell! Speak no more!

Maria.

And must my brother die? Weislingen, it is horrible that I should have to tell thee he is guiltless; that I should be compelled to come as a suppliant to restrain thee from a most fearful murder. Thy soul to its inmost depths is possessed by evil powers. Can this be Adelbert?

Weislingen.

Thou seest—the consuming breath of the grave hath swept over me—my strength sinks in death—I die in misery, and thou comest to drive me to despair. Could I but tell thee all, thy bitterest hate would melt to sorrow and compassion. O Maria! Maria!

Maria.

Weislingen, my brother is pining in a dungeon—the anguish of his wounds—his age—Oh, hadst thou the heart to bring his gray hairs— Weislingen, we should despair.

Weislingen.

Enough!—

[*Rings a hand-bell.*

*Enter*FRANCIS,*in great agitation.*

Francis.

Gracious sir.

Weislingen.

Those papers, Francis. (*He gives them.*WEISLINGEN*tears open a packet and shows*MARIA*a paper.*) Here is thy brother's death-warrant signed!

Maria.

God in heaven!

Weislingen.

And thus I tear it. He shall live! But can I restore what I have destroyed? Weep not so, Francis! Dear youth, my wretchedness lies deeply at thy heart.

[FRANCIS*throws himself at his feet, and clasps his knees.*

Maria.

(*Apart.*) He is ill—very ill. The sight of him rends my heart. I loved him! And now that I again approach him, I feel how dearly—

Weislingen.

Francis, arise and cease to weep—I may recover! While there is life there is hope.

Francis.

You cannot! You must die!

Weislingen.

Must?

Francis.

(*Beside himself.*) Poison! poison!—from your wife! I—I gave it.

[*Rushes out.*

Weislingen.

Follow him, Maria—he is desperate.

[*Exit*MARIA.

Poison from my wife! Alas! alas! I feel it. Torture and death!

Maria.

(Within.) Help! help!

Weislingen.

(Attempts in vain to rise.) God! I cannot.

Maria.

(Re-entering.) He is gone! He threw himself desperately from a window of the hall into the river.

Weislingen.

It is well with him! — Thy brother is out of danger! The other commissioners, especially Seckendorf, are his friends. They will readily allow him to ward himself upon his knightly word. Farewell, Maria! Now go.

Maria.

I will stay with thee — thou poor forsaken one!

Weislingen.

Poor and forsaken indeed! O God, Thou art a terrible avenger! My wife!

Maria.

Remove from thee that thought. Turn thy soul to the throne of mercy.

Weislingen.

Go, thou gentle spirit! leave me to my misery! Horrible! Even thy presence, Maria, even the attendance of my only comforter, is agony.

Maria.

(Aside.) Strengthen me, Heaven! My soul droops with his.

Weislingen.

Alas! alas! Poison from my wife! My Francis seduced by the wretch! She waits — listens to every horse's hoof for the messenger who brings her the news of my death. And thou too, Maria, wherefore art thou come to awaken every slumbering recollection of my sins? Leave me, leave me that I may die!

Maria.

Let me stay! Thou art alone: think I am thy nurse. Forget all. May God forgive thee as freely as I do!

Weislingen.

Thou spirit of love! pray for me! pray for me! My heart is seared.

Maria.

There is forgiveness for thee. — Thou art exhausted.

Weislingen.

I die! I die! and yet I cannot die. In the fearful contest between life and death lie the torments of hell.

Maria.

Heavenly Father, have compassion upon him. Grant him but one token of Thy love, that his heart may be opened to comfort, and his soul to the hope of eternal life, even in the agony of death!

SCENE XI. —

*A narrow Vault dimly illuminated. The*JUDGES OF THE SECRET TRIBUNAL*discovered seated, all muffled in black cloaks.*

Eldest Judge.

Judges of the Secret Tribunal, sworn by the cord and the steel to be inflexible in justice, to judge in secret, and to avenge in secret, like the Deity! Are your hands clean and your hearts pure? Raise them to heaven and cry, — Woe upon evil-doers!

All.

Woe! woe!

Eldest Judge.

Crier, begin the diet of judgment.

Crier.

I cry, I cry for accusation against evil-doers! He whose heart is pure, whose hands are clean to swear by the cord and the steel, let him lift up his voice and call upon the steel and the cord for vengeance! vengeance! vengeance!

Accuser.

(Comes forward.) My heart is pure from misdeed, and my hands are clean from innocent blood: God pardon my sins of thought, and prevent their execution. I raise my hand on high, and cry for vengeance! vengeance! vengeance!

Eldest Judge.

Vengeance upon whom?

Accuser.

I call upon the cord and the steel for vengeance against Adelaide of Weislingen. She has committed adultery and murder. She has poisoned her husband by the hands of his servant—the servant hath slain himself—the husband is dead.

Eldest Judge.

Dost thou swear by the God of truth, that thy accusation is true?

Accuser.

I swear!

Eldest Judge.

Dost thou invoke upon thine own head the punishment of murder and adultery, should thy accusation be found false?

Accuser.

On my head be it.

Eldest Judge.

Your voices?

[*They converse a few minutes in whispers.*

Accuser.

Judges of the Secret Tribunal, what is your sentence upon Adelaide of Weislingen, accused of murder and adultery?

Eldest Judge.

She shall die!—she shall die a bitter and twofold death! By the double doom of the steel and the cord shall she expiate the double crime. Raise your hands to heaven and cry, Woe, woe upon her! Be she delivered into the hands of the avenger.

All.

Woe! woe!

Eldest Judge.

Woe! Avenger, come forth.

[*A man advances.*

Here, take thou the cord and the steel! Within eight days shalt thou blot her out from before the face of heaven: wheresoever thou findest her, down with her into the dust. Judges, ye that judge in secret and avenge in secret like the Deity, keep your hearts from wickedness, and your hands from innocent blood! [*The Scene closes.*

SCENE XII. —

The Court of an Inn.
LERSE*and*MARIA.
Maria.
The horses have rested long enough: we will away, Lerse.
Lerse.
Stay till to-morrow; this is a dreadful night.
Maria.
Lerse, I cannot rest till I have seen my brother. Let us away: the weather is clearing up — we may expect a fair morning.
Lerse.
Be it as you will.

SCENE XIII. —

The Prison at Heilbronn.
GOETZ*and*ELIZABETH.
Elizabeth.
I entreat thee, dear husband, speak to me. Thy silence alarms me; thy spirit consumes thee, pent up within thy breast. Come, let me see thy wounds; they mend daily. In this desponding melancholy I know thee no longer!
Goetz.
Seekest thou Goetz? He is long since gone! Piece by piece have they robbed me of all I held dear — my hand, my property, my

freedom, my good name! My life! of what value is it to me? What news of George? Is Lerse gone to seek him?

Elizabeth.

He is, my love! Be of good cheer; things may yet take a favorable turn.

Goetz.

He whom God hath stricken lifts himself up no more! I best know the load I have to bear.—To misfortune I am inured.— But now it is not Weislingen alone, not the peasants alone, not the death of the emperor, nor my wounds—it is the whole united—. My hour is come! I had hoped it should have been like my life. But His will be done!

Elizabeth.

Wilt thou not eat something?

Goetz.

Nothing, my love! See how the sun shines yonder!

Elizabeth.

It is a fine spring day!

Goetz.

My love, wilt thou ask the keeper's permission for me to walk in his little garden for half an hour, that I may look upon the clear face of heaven, the pure air, and the blessed sun?

Elizabeth.

I will—and he will readily grant it.

SCENE The Last. —

The Prison Garden.
LERSE*and*MARIA.

Maria.

Go in, and see how it stands with them.
[*Exit*LERSE.
*Enter*ELIZABETH*and*KEEPER.

Elizabeth.

(*To the*KEEPER.) God reward your kindness and attention to my husband! (*Exit*KEEPER.) Maria, how hast thou sped?

Maria.

My brother is safe! But my heart is torn asunder. Weislingen is dead! poisoned by his wife. My husband is in danger — the princes are becoming too powerful for him: they say he is surrounded and besieged.

Elizabeth.

Believe not the rumor; and let not Goetz hear it.

Maria.

How is it with him?

Elizabeth.

I feared he would not survive till thy return: the hand of the Lord is heavy on him. And George is dead!

Maria.

George! The gallant boy!

Elizabeth.

When the miscreants were burning Miltenberg his master sent him to check their villany. A body of cavalry charged upon them: had they all behaved as George, they must all have had as clear a conscience. Many were killed, and George among them; he died the death of a warrior.

Maria.

Does Goetz know it?

Elizabeth.

We conceal it from him. He questions me ten times a day concerning him, and sends me as often to see what is become of him. I fear to give his heart this last wound.

Maria.

O God! what are the hopes of this world?

*Enter*GOETZ, LERSE*and*KEEPER.

Goetz.

Almighty God! how lovely it is beneath Thy heaven! How free! The trees put forth their buds, and all the world awakes to hope. — Farewell, my children! my roots are cut away, my strength totters to the grave.

Elizabeth.

Shall I not send Lerse to the convent for thy son, that thou may'st once more see and bless him?

Goetz.

Let him be; he needs not my blessing, he is holier than I. — Upon our wedding-day, Elizabeth, could I have thought I should die thus! — My old father blessed us, and prayed for a succession of noble and gallant sons — God, Thou hast not heard him. I am the last. — Lerse, thy countenance cheers me in the hour of death more than in our most daring fights: then, my spirit encouraged all of you; now, thine supports me. — Oh, that I could but once more see George, and sun myself in his look! You turn away and weep. He is dead? George is dead? Then die, Goetz! Thou hast outlived thyself, outlived the noblest of thy servants. — How died he? Alas! they took him among the incendiaries, and he has been executed?

Elizabeth.

No! he was slain at Miltenberg! while fighting like a lion for his freedom.

Goetz.

God be praised! He was the kindest youth under the sun, and one of the bravest. — Now release my soul. My poor wife! I leave thee in a wicked world. Lerse, forsake her not! Look your hearts more carefully than your doors. The age of fraud is at hand, treachery will reign unchecked. The worthless will gain the ascendency by cunning, and the noble will fall into their net. Maria, may God restore thy husband to thee! may he not fall the deeper for having risen so high! Selbitz is dead, and the good emperor, and my George — give me a draught of water! — Heavenly air! Freedom! freedom!

[*He dies.*

Elizabeth.

Freedom is above! above — with thee! The world is a prison-house.

Maria.

Noble man! Woe to this age that rejected thee!

Lerse.
And woe to the future, that shall misjudge thee.